HOUGHTON MIFFLIN HARCOURT

WRITE SOURCE

SkillsBook

GREAT SOURCE.

 HOUGHTON MIFFLIN HARCOURT

A Few Words About the *Write Source SkillsBook*

Before you begin . . .

The *SkillsBook* provides you with opportunities to practice editing and proofreading skills. *Write Source* contains guidelines, examples, and models to help you complete your work in the *SkillsBook*.

Each *SkillsBook* activity includes brief instruction on the topic and examples showing how to complete that activity. You will be directed to the page numbers in *Write Source* for additional information and examples.

The "Proofreading Activities" focus on punctuation, the mechanics of writing, usage, and spelling. The "Sentence Activities" provide practice in sentence combining and in correcting common sentence problems. The "Language Activities" highlight parts of speech.

Many exercises end with a **Next Step** activity. This feature provides follow-up work that will help you apply what you have learned to your own writing.

Printed in the U.S.A.

ISBN 978-0-547-48443-3

9 10 0982 17 16 15 14

4500470808 A B C D E F G

Table of Contents

Proofreading Activities

Using Punctuation

Periods 1 and 2 3
End Punctuation 7
Commas Between Items in a Series 9
Commas in Letter Writing 11
Commas to Keep Numbers Clear 12
Commas in Dates and Addresses 13
Commas in Compound Sentences 15
Commas to Set Off a Speaker's Words 17
Commas After an Introductory Word 19
Commas After a Group of Words 21
Apostrophes 1, 2, and 3 23
Quotation Marks 1 and 2 29
Quotation Marks, Underlining, and Italics to Punctuate Titles 33
Colons 35
Hyphens 37
Parentheses 38
Punctuation Review 39

Checking Mechanics

Capitalizing Proper Nouns 41
Capitalizing Official Titles 43
Capitalizing First Words 44
Capitalizing Titles 45
Capitalizing Historical Periods 46
Capitalizing Geographic Names and Places 47
Capitalization Review 49
Plurals 1 and 2 51
Writing Numbers 55
Using Abbreviations 56
State Abbreviations 57
Mixed Review 59

Proofreading Activities

Checking Your Spelling

Spelling and Alphabetizing 61
Spelling and Silent Letters 63
Spelling Sorts 65

Using the Right Word

Using the Right Word 1, 2, 3, 4, 5, 6, and 7 67
Using the Right Word Review 74

Sentence Activities

Sentence Basics

Simple and Complete Subjects and Predicates 77
Subject of a Sentence 79
Predicate of a Sentence 81
Subject and Predicate Review 83
Simple and Compound Sentences 1 and 2 85
Simple Sentences and Subject-Verb Agreement 89
Compound Sentences and Subject-Verb Agreement 91

Sentence Problems

Sentence Fragments 1, 2, and 3 93
Run-On Sentences 1 and 2 97

Sentence Combining

Combining Sentences with a Key Word 101
Combining Sentences with a Series of Words or Phrases 1 and 2 103
Combining Sentences with Compound Subjects and Verbs 1 and 2 107
Sentence Combining Review 1 and 2 111

Language Activities

Nouns

Nouns 117
Common and Proper Nouns 119
Singular and Plural Nouns 121
Possessive Nouns 1 and 2 123

Pronouns

Personal Pronouns 1 and 2 125
Pronouns: I and Me, They and Them 129
Possessive Pronouns 131

Verbs

Action and Linking Verbs 133
Helping Verbs 135
Verb Review 1 136
Verb Tenses 1, 2, and 3 137
Regular Verbs 143
Singular and Plural Verbs 145
Irregular Verbs 147
Verb Review 2 149

Adjectives and Adverbs

Adjectives 1, 2, and 3 151
Proper Adjectives 155
Compound Adjectives 156
Forms of Adjectives 157
Adverbs 1 and 2 159

Prepositions, Conjunctions, Transitions

Prepositions and Prepositional Phrases 163
Conjunctions 165
Transitions 166
Parts of Speech Review 1 and 2 167

1

Proofreading Activities

The activities in this section include sentences that need to be checked for spelling, mechanics, and usage. Each activity includes a link to a page or pages in *Write Source* to be used as a guide for the activity.

Using Punctuation	**3**
Checking Mechanics	**41**
Checking Your Spelling	**61**
Using the Right Word	**67**

Name ______________________________

Periods 1

A **period** is just a little dot, but it has a lot of important uses.

- For one thing, a period is used at the end of a sentence that makes a **statement.**

  Frogs begin their lives in the water.
  Later, they live on land.
  Frogs are amphibians.

- A period is also used at the end of a **request.**

  Please look up "amphibian" in the dictionary.
  Find out what the word means.

Put an *S* in front of each statement, and put an *R* in front of each request. End each sentence with a period. The first one has been done for you.

S **1.** Most frogs are expert swimmers.

_____ **2.** Frogs get much of their power from their strong back legs

_____ **3.** Do the frog kick next time you are in the water

_____ **4.** Draw your legs up to your sides

_____ **5.** Then push them straight back

_____ **6.** You will move forward just as a frog does

_____ **7.** You might enjoy swimming this way

_____ **8.** Frogs wouldn't swim in any other way

2 **The following paragraph has nine sentences in it. Find the nine sentences. Put a capital letter at the beginning of each one and a period at the end of each one. The first sentence has been done for you.**

some frogs have homes that are high off the ground these frogs live in trees tree frogs like leafy homes many tree frogs are green not all of them are green some are yellow, red, or orange others have stripes and spots tree frogs live in all parts of the world you may have some in your neighborhood

Next Step **Write two sentences. In the first one, state something that a frog can do. In the second one, tell a friend to do something that a frog does.**

1. *Statement:* ______________________________

____

____

2. *Request:* ______________________________

____

____

Name ______________________________

Periods 2

Put a **period** after an initial in a person's name. Also use a period after an abbreviation and to separate dollars and cents.

Carl B. Picklefoot   M. Jennifer Jump
Mr. Picklefoot   Foster Ave.
$1.25 $11.00

1 **Put periods after the initials in Samantha's name. Then write your name in all of these ways.**

Samantha R ______________________

Samantha J Rowe ______________________

S J Rowe ______________________

S J R ______________________

2 **Put periods after the abbreviations in these sentences.**

1. Where does Mr Brown live?
2. He used to live on W Water St , but now he has moved.
3. His new home is on E Carver Ave , next door to Ms Trout.
4. Ms Trout is a dentist, so she is also Dr Trout.
5. One of Mr Brown's other neighbors is Lt O'Malley, a police officer.
6. Many of the homes on E Carver Ave were built by J J Builders.

3

Add 11 periods where they belong in the paragraph below. The first sentence has been done for you.

Mr. Henry J. Picklefoot went to E. Lancaster to visit his cousin, Ms. Mary W. Bristle. Ms Bristle works at a movie theater in E Lancaster. The theater is on W Broad St , just past J J Pollacco's Pizza Palace. While Ms Bristle was working, Mr Picklefoot went to three movies. Each one cost $7 00. The next day, Mr Picklefoot decided to go back home to W Lancaster. He had seen enough movies.

4

Write the following amounts as numbers with dollar signs and periods to separate dollars and cents.

1. Ten dollars and twenty-nine cents ______________
2. One hundred dollars and two cents ______________
3. Two dollars and seventy-three cents ______________
4. Forty dollars and no cents ______________
5. Ninety-nine dollars and ninety-nine cents ______________
6. Eighteen dollars and thirty-six cents ______________

Next Step **Write two names that include abbreviations or initials. Write two numbers with dollars and cents. (You can find this information in a magazine or newspaper.) Then write two sentences using these names and numbers.**

Name ______________________________

End Punctuation

- A **question mark** follows a question.

  Do you want broccoli for supper?

- An **exclamation point** follows a word or sentence that shows strong feeling.

  Wow! That's a great idea!

- A **period** follows a statement or a request.

  I'm not sure I heard you. Say that again.

Put a period, a question mark, or an exclamation point at the end of each of these sentences.

1. What's good about broccoli ________
2. Broccoli is rich in vitamins ________
3. It tastes great ________
4. It has a pretty green color ________
5. The home gardener finds it easy to grow ________
6. Why doesn't everyone eat broccoli ________
7. I like it with cheese sauce ________
8. Who likes it raw ________
9. I do ________ I do ________
10. Broccoli is definitely my favorite vegetable ________

2 Put a question mark, an exclamation point, or a period at the end of each sentence in this paragraph.

My favorite vegetable is carrots They're so sweet Do you know how my little brother eats carrots He puts them in rolls and eats them like hot dogs It's gross What is your favorite vegetable Do you like carrots, too

Next Step **Write three sentences about one of the vegetables listed below. One sentence should make a statement or request, another sentence should ask a question, and the third one should express strong feeling.**

eggplant cabbage asparagus squash corn

1. *Statement:* ______________________________

____

____

2. *Question:* ______________________________

____

____

3. *Exclamation:* ______________________________

____

Name ______________________________

Commas Between Items in a Series

- Use commas between words in a series.

  Most desks are full of papers, pencils, and books.

- Use commas between phrases in a series.

  My dad uses solar calculators, felt-tip pens, and sticky notes.

In each sentence, put commas between the words and phrases in the series.

1. My mom's desk is covered with letters bills and pictures.
2. Paper clips safety pins and thumbtacks are in a jar.
3. She keeps rulers scissors and a plant on a shelf.
4. The top drawer holds stickers rubber bands two checkbooks and three notepads.
5. The bottom drawer contains spiral notebooks file folders and old letters.
6. She keeps pencils pens and markers in a can that I made in school.
7. A dictionary a world atlas and two telephone directories are placed on another shelf.

Next Step Make a list of things you have in your desk or locker.

Now write a paragraph about the things in your desk or locker. Your sentences should include words or phrases in a series. Begin with this topic sentence: Please don't open this desk!

Name ______________________________

Commas in Letter Writing

Use a comma after a greeting in a letter and after the closing.

- A postcard

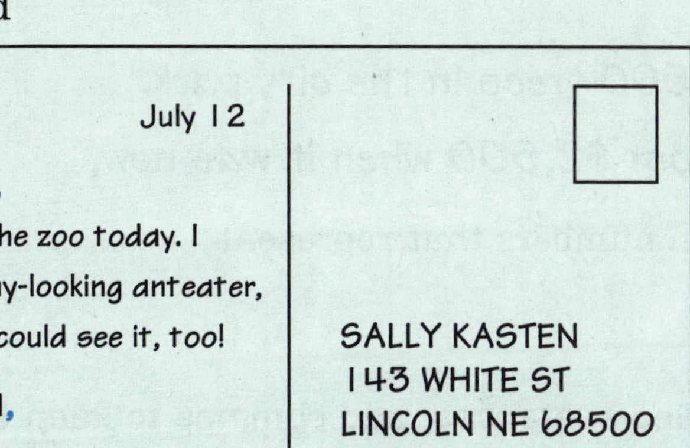

1 **Write your own postcard message below. Be sure to add a date and sign your name. Use commas correctly.**

Name ______________________________

Write Source Link
466

Commas to Keep Numbers Clear

Commas are used in numbers to make them easier to read. If there are four or more numbers, use a comma.

There are about 1,500 trees in the city park.

That old car only cost $2,500 when it was new.

Hint: Don't use commas in numbers that represent a year (1776, 2010).

In the following sentences, add commas to keep the numbers clear. If the number does not need a comma, circle the number. The first one has been done for you.

1. Our teacher told me that our school has 1,728 students.
2. Some United States Navy ships have a crew of 5000 people.
3. The principal said that 300 parents came to our talent show.
4. Someone gave $2500 to the school for new drums.
5. My mother paid $25 for my new backpack.
6. The wall near the school playground has 3200 bricks in it.

Next Step **Add commas to the numbers below where needed.**

1. the year 2000
2. 290 boxes
3. 3250 people
4. 1475 tickets
5. $4555
6. 2312 computers

Name

Commas in Dates and Addresses

1 Write the information below for three of your classmates or friends. Be sure to put a comma between the city and state of each address and between the day and year of each birth date.

Name ______________________

Address ______________________

City, State, ZIP ______________________

Birth Date ______________________

Name ______________________

Address ______________________

City, State, ZIP ______________________

Birth Date ______________________

Name ______________________

Address ______________________

City, State, ZIP ______________________

Birth Date ______________________

2 Complete each invitation below. Use the names and addresses from the first page in this activity. (Feel free to decorate the invitations.)

Surprise Party

Please come to a surprise party for

____

Date: ______________________________

Time: ______________________________

Address: ______________________________

____

Neighborhood Picnic

Please join ______________________________

for an afternoon of fun.

Address: ______________________________

____

Date: ______________________________

Time: ______________________________

Name ______________________________

Commas in Compound Sentences

Use a **comma** before the coordinating conjunction in a compound sentence. Some common conjunctions are *and, but,* and *or.*

I study plants in school, and I know a lot about them.

I've read about the Venus flytrap, but I've never seen one.

1 **Underline the coordinating conjunction in each of these compound sentences. Put a comma before each conjunction.**

1. Most plants get their food from soil but some plants eat insects.
2. The Venus flytrap grows in swamps and it really is a trap for flies.
3. The flytrap looks harmless but it is a danger zone for bugs.
4. The leaves are like traps and they actually have teeth!
5. An insect lands on a flytrap's leaf and the leaf snaps shut.
6. The insect is trapped and it can't get away.
7. Venus flytraps are grown in plant stores or they grow wild.
8. You can feed your Venus flytrap bugs but you shouldn't feed it meat.
9. Meat has salt in it and Venus flytraps don't like salt.

2

Combine each pair of simple sentences to make a compound sentence. Put a comma before the coordinating conjunction. The first one has been done for you.

1. Computers are fast.
   They are fun to use.

   Computers are fast, and they are fun to use.

2. Robin wants to use her new computer.
   She does not know how to turn it on.

   ____

   ____

3. She needs help fast.
   She will cry.

   ____

   ____

4. Robin asks Ms. Kadiddle.
   She says she will help.

   ____

   ____

Next Step **Use a compound sentence with a coordinating conjunction to tell a partner about using a computer.**

Name ______________________________

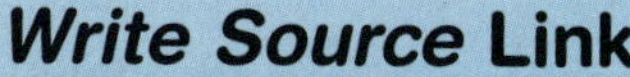

Commas to Set Off a Speaker's Words

Use a **comma** to set off the exact words of a speaker from the rest of the sentence.

Ms. Ayala asked, "Who remembers the story of the wolf and the kid?"

"I think I do," answered Jamal.

Put commas where they are needed in these sentences.

1. "It was about a mother goat who went to get food for her kid" Jamal said.
2. "That's the beginning" said Sam. "Then the mother told the kid to lock the door and not let anyone in."
3. "Next a wolf knocks on the door and talks sweet like the mother" Jamal said.
4. Sam continued "The kid peeks through the window and sees the wolf."
5. "And he doesn't let the wolf in" said Jamal.
6. Ms. Ayala said "What lesson can you learn from this story?"
7. "Mothers know best" laughed Sam and Jamal.

Next Step Write one more thing Ms. Ayala could have said about the story. Be sure to use a comma where it is needed.

2 Put commas where they are needed in the following sentences.

1. "Let's think of other fables we've read" said the teacher.
2. Jan replied "I remember the one about the ant and the grasshopper."
3. "Oh, that's where the ant does all the work and the grasshopper is lazy" said Amy.
4. "Yes" said Jan. "The ant saved food for the winter, while the grasshopper wasted time."
5. "There's a lesson there" said the teacher.
6. Amy said "I think it means we should do our work on time."
7. "Good thinking" said the teacher.

Next Step Write one more thing the teacher might say. Use a comma and quotation marks in your sentence.

Name ________________________________

Commas After an Introductory Word

- Use a **comma** to set off the name of a person or group being spoken to.

  Class, we're starting an all-drum band.

- Use a comma to set off an interjection.

  Gosh, that will make a loud noise!

1 **Add commas where they are needed in these sentences.**

1. Josh you play the conga drum.
2. Yolanda you take the tom-tom.
3. Tony here's a tabla drum for you.
4. Wow you sure can play the big bass drum, Elle.
5. Help I can't lift this big drum.
6. Look that drum is taller than I am.
7. George can you play a bongo drum?
8. Carla you play the triangle.
9. Our teacher said, "Wait I want everyone to stay after practice."

Next Step Imagine that your class is going to have a band with many different instruments. Write four sentences, each telling a person to play an instrument. (Choose from the instruments below, or come up with your own.) Make sure to use commas correctly. One has been done for you.

maracas	guitar	flute
tambourine	banjo	piano

1. Todd, you play the tambourine.

2. ______________________________

3. ______________________________

4. ______________________________

5. ______________________________

Name ______________________________

Commas After a Group of Words

- Use a **comma** to set off an introductory group of words. Often, an introductory group of words is a prepositional phrase. A prepositional phrase is a preposition and the word or words that come after it.

After school, I play with my friends.

When it gets too dark, we all head for home.

Add commas where they are needed in the following sentences. Three sentences do not need commas.

1. Because it was dark the playground was closed.
2. I rode my bike around the block.
3. When my mom came home I gave her a big hug.
4. After supper we played catch.
5. I like to drink hot cocoa before bedtime.
6. While I brushed my teeth my dad talked about our fishing trip.
7. Before I went to sleep I read my favorite book.
8. During the night I dreamed about catching huge fish.
9. In the morning my mom asked me if I wanted sardines for breakfast.
10. I think I was still dreaming.

2

Complete the sentences below. Make sure you add a comma after the introductory words. The first one has been done for you.

1. When lightning flashes in the sky, I listen for the loud boom of the thunder.

2. After the rain starts falling ________________

3. During the storm ________________

4. Because my dog doesn't like thunder ________________

5. Until the sun shines again ________________

Next Step **Tell a partner what you do during a storm. Use prepositions and prepositional phrases in your answer.**

Name ______________________________

Apostrophes 1

An **apostrophe** is used in the spelling of a contraction. The apostrophe takes the place of one or more letters.

Two Words	Contraction
did not	didn't
you are	you're
I am	I'm

apostrophes

1 **Write a contraction for each word or word pair in the list. Then rewrite each sentence, replacing the words in bold letters with a contraction.**

Two Words	Contraction
is not	______________
it is	______________
do not	______________
they are	______________
cannot	______________

1. Mary **cannot** sing. Mary can't sing.
2. Jake **is not** singing. ______________
3. **They are** both not singing. ______________
4. **It is** time for you to sing. ______________
5. But I **do not** want to. ______________

2 Write contractions for the following word pairs.

Two Words	Contraction	Two Words	Contraction
1. it is; it has	________	8. will not	________
2. they will	________	9. I would	________
3. do not	________	10. who is	________
4. I am	________	11. there is	________
5. I have	________	12. could not	________
6. is not	________	13. was not	________
7. you are	________	14. did not	________

3 In each sentence below, write a contraction to replace the words in bold.

1. **They will** be riding six white horses when she comes. ________
2. **It is** just like a magic penny. ________
3. But the cat came back: it just **could not** stay away. ________
4. If **you are** happy and you know it, clap your hands. ________
5. **There is** a hole in the bottom of the sea. ________
6. **I have** been working on the railroad. ________
7. **Who is** afraid of the big, bad wolf? ________
8. **I am** a little teapot short and stout. ________

Next Step The sentences above are lines from songs. Can you sing any of them?

Name ______________________________

Apostrophes 2

An **apostrophe** plus an **s** is added to a singular noun to show ownership. (Singular means "one.")

the girl's bike (The bike belongs to the girl.)
the cat's whiskers
(The whiskers belong to the cat.)

1

In each sentence, put an apostrophe in the word that tells who the gerbil belongs to. The first one has been done for you.

1. Chester's gerbil likes leaf lettuce.
2. I think LaJoys gerbil is the cutest.
3. Where is the teachers gerbil?
4. Mollys gerbil is under my desk!
5. My neighbors gerbil stays in a cage.

2

In each sentence, draw a line under the word that tells who the hat belongs to. Draw one of the hats in the box.

1. Who has the baby's hat?
2. Mr. Dandelion's hat is yellow.
3. Look at Roger's hat!
4. Did you see Kathy's red hat?
5. Rocky Stark's hat is black.

3

Combine each set of words into a possessive phrase. Then write an interesting sentence using the phrase. Make sure to use apostrophes correctly. The first one has been done for you.

1. Betty ➤ house Betty's house ______

   I went to Betty's house to play. ______

2. my sister ➤ pony ______

   ______

3. our dog ➤ name ______

   ______

4. a clown ➤ face ______

   ______

5. Mr. Brown ➤ car ______

   ______

6. a bluebird ➤ house ______

   ______

7. Shauna ➤ desk ______

   ______

Next Step **Exchange your sentences with a classmate. Check the apostrophes in your partner's work.**

Name ___________________________

Apostrophes 3

- Add **'s** to a singular noun to show ownership. (Singular means "one.")

  the dog's house

- Add an apostrophe after a plural noun ending in **s**. (Plural means "more than one.")

  the dogs' houses

Add an apostrophe in each phrase below to show ownership. In the blank, tell if the phrase shows singular or plural possession. The first one has been done for you.

1. Maryanne has one hamster in a cage. You write . . .

   the hamster's cage **singular possession**

2. Claudia has a cage with three hamsters in it. You write . . .

   the hamsters cage ______________________

3. You have a rabbit. The rabbit lives in a hutch. You write . . .

   the rabbits hutch ______________________

4. Your brother gets a rabbit, so you have two rabbits. You write . . .

   the rabbits hutch ______________________

5. The rabbits have babies. You have to get another hutch. You write . . .

   the rabbits hutches ______________________

2

Put a possessive singular noun in the blank to complete each sentence. The first sentence has been done for you.

1. Madeline's dog ate my lunch.
2. My ______________ dog likes potato chips.
3. ______________ dog barked at me.
4. Where is ______________ little dog?
5. I have to walk ______________ dog for a week.

Next Step

Below is a list of names and the things that belong to each person or group. Combine the two words into a possessive phrase. Then write an interesting sentence using the phrase. The first one has been done for you.

1. Katie ➤ roller skates Katie's roller skates

   Katie's roller skates have lightning bolts painted on them.

2. Mr. Frank ➤ cane ______________

   ____

3. Dolly ➤ wig ______________

   ____

4. the Dolphins ➤ helmets ______________

   ____

5. Diana ➤ gowns ______________

   ____

Name ______________________________

Quotation Marks 1

Write Source Link

476

One way to show what people say to each other is to use speech balloons.

Why didn't you call me back last night?

I'm sorry. We got home very late.

Another way to show what people say is to use **quotation marks.** The quotation marks set off the exact words of the speaker.

Tom said, "Why didn't you call me back last night?"
"I'm sorry. We got home very late," Les answered.

1 **Read the words in the speech balloons below. Then, in the sentences that follow, put quotation marks before and after the exact words that Tom and Les said.**

I wanted to ask if you could sleep over Saturday night.

I hope I can. I'll ask my mom.

Tom said, I wanted to ask if you could sleep over Saturday night.

I hope I can. I'll ask my mom, said Les.

2 **Read the speech balloons that follow. Then, in the space below, write what Tom and Les said, using quotation marks correctly in your sentences.**

Tom said, ____

____

____

Les replied, ____

____

____

Next Step **It's the next day. Tom and Les see each other again. Now you decide what they say. Make sure to use quotation marks correctly.**

____

____

____

____

Name

Quotation Marks 2

When you write **dialogue**, you can name the speaker at the beginning of the sentence, at the end of the sentence, or in the middle of the sentence.

- When the speaker is named at the **beginning** of the sentence, use a comma and quotation marks like this:

  Carla said, "I'm going to camp this summer."

- When the speaker is named at the **end** of the sentence, use a comma and quotation marks like this:

  "Late at night, we tell ghost stories," said Camy.

- When the speaker is named in the **middle** of the sentence, use commas and quotation marks like this:

  "Camp starts July 5," Carla said, "and we stay for two weeks."

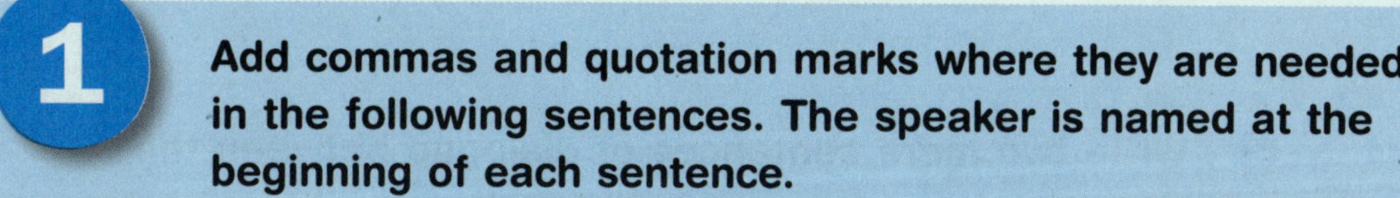

1 **Add commas and quotation marks where they are needed in the following sentences. The speaker is named at the beginning of each sentence.**

1. Camy said I'm going, too.
2. Josh said Won't you miss your parents?
3. Carla answered Yes, but we'll still have fun.
4. Josh asked What are you going to take?
5. Carla said I'm taking a lot of shorts and T-shirts.

2

Add commas and quotation marks in the sentences below. The speaker is named at the end of each sentence.

1. The ghost stories always scare me a little Camy said.
2. I'd be scared, too said Josh.
3. Aw, they're only fake stories said Carla.

3

Add commas and quotation marks in the following sentences. The speaker is named in the middle of each sentence.

1. This summer said Carla I'm going to learn to dive.
2. I can dive Camy said but not headfirst.
3. If it's not headfirst said Josh it's not a dive.
4. If it's belly first Josh said it's a belly flop!

Next Step **Write two more sentences of dialogue between the campers. Use commas and quotation marks correctly to punctuate your dialogue.**

____

____

____

____

____

____

Name ________________________________

Quotation Marks, Underlining, and Italics to Punctuate Titles

When you write, put quotation marks around titles of songs, short stories, and poems. Underline the titles of books, movies, TV programs, plays, and magazines and the names of ships and aircraft. (Use italics instead of underlining if you write with a computer). Also, remember to use these rules when you cite references on a works-cited page.

We sang "The Star-Spangled Banner" before the game.

Marie read the poem "Clouds on a Windy Day."

Al liked the story "Babbling Brook."

I watched the movie *Bambi* with my little sister. (or Bambi)

I enjoyed reading the magazine *Cricket*. (or Cricket)

Punctuate the titles used in the sentences below.

1. Ali likes to read the magazine National Geographic.
2. My friends watched the movie Peter Pan.
3. Our class read the short story The Mountain.
4. We sang the song Row, Row, Row Your Boat five times.
5. My mother bought the book Airborn.
6. Jamie likes the TV show called Bill Nye the Science Guy.
7. Ona, Cloud Rider is a great short story.
8. The Nina, Pinta, and Santa Maria were Columbus' ships.

In each sentence below, punctuate the title with quotation marks or underlining.

1. Yoko went to see the movie The Incredibles.
2. The Ranger Rick magazine is filled with facts about animals.
3. Sylvia's dad bought her a book called The Tale of Despereaux.
4. Everybody sang Old MacDonald Had a Farm.
5. Joann says she likes the Muppets on Sesame Street.
6. Sammy smiles when he reads the poem Three Words.
7. Phil's family bought Spider-Man 2 in the DVD version.
8. Flat Stanley is one of Josie's favorite books.
9. Do you like this magazine? It's called Highlights.

Next Step Write two sentences. Each should include the title of a song, a book, a movie, or a magazine. Be sure to punctuate the titles correctly.

Name ____________________________

Colons

- Use a **colon** after the salutation of a business letter.

  Dear Ms. Cosby: Dear Sir:

- Use a colon between the hours and the minutes in a number that shows time.

  1:15 12:30

Add colons as they are needed in the business letter below.

Dear Mayor Hudson

I am writing to let you know about our neighborhood's "Cleanup Day." It will take place on Saturday, April 17, from 1 0 0 0 a.m. to 4 0 0 p.m. City trucks will be needed at the following times and places:

1 1 3 0 a.m.	City trucks needed to begin picking up bagged trash. It will be placed at street corners throughout the neighborhood.
1 2 0 0 noon	Lunch will be donated by El Taco Grande.
4 0 0 p.m.	City trucks needed to pick up brush cleared at Green Bayou Park. Brush will be piled at the park entrance.

Thank you for your help with this project.

Sincerely,

Matt Stone

Matt Stone

2

Below are the beginnings of some business letters. Students wrote these letters to confirm plans for field trips. Add colons where they are needed in the letters.

1. Dear Fire Chief Wilson

Our class is looking forward to visiting the fire station next Monday from 9 3 0 until 1 1 0 0 a.m.

2. Dear Ms. Stephanopoulos

Thank you for inviting us to visit your bakery on Friday between 1 0 3 0 a.m. and 1 2 0 0 noon.

3. Dear Ms. Kennedy

Our class is excited about visiting the TV station from 1 0 0 until 2 0 0 p.m. next Friday.

4. Dear Mr. Alvarez

We are looking forward to our tour of the stadium next Thursday between 1 1 0 0 a.m. and 1 2 3 0 p.m.

Next Step **Write the beginning of a letter about an upcoming field trip. Write your letter to someone who works at a place you would like to visit. (Make up his or her name.)**

Name ______________________________

Hyphens

A hyphen is used to divide a word into syllables. Do this when you run out of room at the end of a line. A dictionary is helpful if you're not sure how to divide a word.

drag-on-fly

I ran outside when I saw the dragonfly on the porch.

1

Divide the words below by using a hyphen between the syllables.

1. kitten ______________________
2. picture ______________________
3. wagon ______________________
4. people ______________________
5. music ______________________
6. helpless ______________________
7. kitchen ______________________
8. hyphen ______________________
9. travel ______________________
10. window ______________________

Name ______________________________

Write Source Link
482

Parentheses

You can use parentheses to add information to your writing.

Use two nails (two inches long) for each side of the box.

Yesterday, I spotted an unusual bird (a brown creeper).

1 **In the sentences below, add parentheses where they are needed.**

1. Mike read about birds in the encyclopedia volume 2.
2. Lee the second boy on the right has three dogs.
3. Store the footballs in the locker green box behind the door.
4. You can read the poem in this book see chapter 3.
5. Reg's house is on Water Street check my map.
6. To paint the model, follow the directions see the back of the box.

Next Step **Write a sentence about the weather that includes parentheses to add information.**

____

____

____

Name ______________________________

Write Source Link
463–483

Punctuation Review

This activity is a review of punctuation marks.

1 **Fill in the blanks in the following sentences. Make sure to use punctuation marks correctly.**

1. Today's date is ______________________________ .

2. My school's name is ______________________________ .

My school is in this city and state:

____

3. School starts at __________ a.m., and it ends at __________ p.m.

4. Our class is studying ______________________________

______________________________ and ______________________________ .

5. Our teacher's name is ______________________________ .

2 **Fill in the blanks in the following sentences. Show each speaker's exact words. Make sure to use commas and quotation marks correctly.**

1. My teacher asked me ______________________________

____

2. I answered ______________________________

____

3 **In the letter below, add the needed punctuation (commas, periods, parentheses, hyphens, and so on).**

April 23 2011

Dear Ramos

After I called you last week I watched the movie Robots The trip through the robot city was amazing. Did you see that movie Josie said that more than 500 kids in our town have seen it. Thats a lot of kids When you come to visit me in July maybe we can rent the movie. I would like to see it again.

Im working on a model ship see the drawing on the back of this letter. It is a nuclear submarine. Its the newest sub marine called the Seawolf. My stepfather is helping me put it together. I will paint it black rust and silver.

I have to go do my homework now. I hope you have fun playing soccer. Lets practice kicking goals when youre here.

Your friend

Brian

Name ______________________________

Capitalizing Proper Nouns

A **proper noun** names a specific person, place, thing, or idea. A proper noun is always capitalized.

Mary

St. Louis

Strawberry Festival

1 Write two proper nouns for each category.

1. city Houston Springfield
2. holiday ______ ______
3. school ______ ______
4. ocean ______ ______
5. person ______ ______
6. park ______ ______

2 Write an interesting sentence using at least two of the proper nouns in your list. Then tell a partner a sentence using two other proper nouns.

____

____

____

____

3 Fill in the missing days and months in the two charts below. Remember that days and months are capitalized.

Days of the Week

1. Monday
2. ______
3. Wednesday
4. ______
5. ______
6. Saturday
7. ______

Months of the Year

1. ______
2. February
3. ______
4. April
5. ______
6. ______
7. ______
8. August
9. ______
10. October
11. ______
12. December

Next Step Tell your answers to the following questions to a partner.

1. What day and month is it today?
2. In what month were you born?
3. What is your favorite day of the week?

Name

Capitalizing Official Titles

Always capitalize **official titles** that are used with names. Do not capitalize the title if it is used instead of the name.

President George Washington
Mayor Mike Martinez

For each sentence, use an official title when naming each person. Be sure to use capitalization correctly.

1. Write a sentence naming the mayor of your city.

2. Write a sentence with the full name of your doctor.

3. Write a sentence with your name as if you were the governor.

4. Write a sentence naming the principal of your school.

5. Write a sentence about your favorite president.

Name

Capitalizing First Words

- Always capitalize the **first word** in a sentence.

  My heart is a muscle.

  Can you hear it beat?

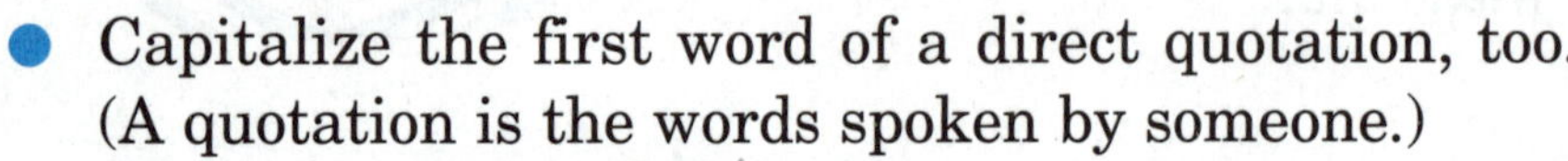

- Capitalize the first word of a direct quotation, too. (A quotation is the words spoken by someone.)

  She said, "Only I can hear it."

1 **Add capital letters where they are needed in the sentences below. The first one has been done for you.**

1. the expert said, "every animal has a pulse rate."
2. it is measured in heartbeats per minute.
3. big animals have slower pulse rates than little animals.
4. find your pulse.
5. "how fast does your heart beat?" he asked.
6. she answered, "my heartbeat is not as fast as a baby's."
7. count the number of times your heart beats in one minute.
8. the average person's heart beats 72 times a minute.
9. runners may have heart rates as low as 35 beats per minute.
10. that's so low!

Name ______________________________

Capitalizing Titles

Capitalize the first word of the **title** of a book or magazine, the last word, and every important word in between.

The Biggest Pancake Ever **(book title)**

Follow these rules for words in the middle of a title.

- Don't capitalize articles *(a, an, the).*
- Don't capitalize short prepositions *(to, with, by, for).*
- Don't capitalize conjunctions *(and, but).*

Tea with Milk (book)

Amelia and Eleanor Go for a Ride (book)

Write the titles using capital letters in the right places. Because these are names of books and magazines, underline them. The first one has been done for you.

1. the cat and the fiddle The Cat and the Fiddle
2. penny pollard's letters ______________________________
3. i'm in charge of celebrations ______________________________
4. the dragon's boy ______________________________
5. song of the trees ______________________________
6. ranger rick ______________________________
7. highlights for children ______________________________

Name ____________________

Capitalizing Historical Periods

Capitalize each word in the name of a **historical** period. A historical period is a length of time that can be identified by events that happened or existed during that time.

1 **Write the historical periods using capital letters correctly. The first one has been done for you.**

1. space age Space Age
2. ice age ____________________
3. computer age ____________________
4. ancient greece ____________________
5. electric age ____________________
6. iron age ____________________
7. dark ages ____________________
8. golden age ____________________

Name ______________________________

Capitalizing Geographic Names and Places

The names of specific rivers, lakes, mountains, cities, states, countries, streets, roads, planets, and highways should be capitalized.

1 Write three geographic names and places in each of the columns. Be sure to use capital letters correctly. (You may want to work on this activity with a partner.)

Rivers	Lakes
______________	______________
______________	______________
______________	______________

Cities	States
______________	______________
______________	______________
______________	______________

Streets/Avenues	Planets
______________	______________
______________	______________
______________	______________

2 **Capitalize the geographic names in these sentences. The numbers in parentheses tell you how many capital letters you need to change. The first sentence has been done for you.**

1. The town of red lion, pennsylvania, is on the susquehanna river. *(5)*

2. If you're looking for lake old wives, you'll find it in canada. *(4)*

3. The hungry horse reservoir is in montana. *(4)*

4. The snake river forms part of the border between idaho and oregon. *(4)*

5. There's a town in arkansas called bad knob. *(3)*

6. In ohio you'll find mount healthy. *(3)*

7. If you ever go to laredo, texas, you might see the rio grande river. *(5)*

8. When pumpkin creek joins the tongue river, they flow into the yellowstone river. *(6)*

9. In new jersey you'll find a city called orange. *(3)*

10. You'll find lake cadibarrawirracanna in australia. *(3)*

11. The brazos river flows through texas. *(3)*

Name ___________________________

Capitalization Review

This activity is a review of capitalization.

Add capital letters in the following paragraphs. Also answer the question after each pargraph.

Rub It Out

in 1770 during the industrial revolution, an englishman named joseph priestley was traveling in south america. he gathered some of the juice coming from the trees. he found that it would rub out pencil marks. he called it rubber.

What are three things that are made of rubber?

________________ ________________ ________________

Blast It

in sweden, a man named alfred nobel invented a blasting material he called dynamite. miners often use dynamite. money he earned from the invention now goes to people who win the nobel prize. one winner of the prize is president barack obama.

Why do miners use dynamite?

____

2 Here are two more paragraphs to capitalize. Also answer the question at the end of each paragraph.

Weave It

long ago, empress si ling-chi was sipping tea in china. a caterpillar cocoon fell into her cup. she unwound the cocoon and said, “it’s made of a long thread. what will happen if I have it woven into cloth?” that’s how chinese silk was discovered. silk was used as money during the han dynasty period.

What are two things that are made of silk?

____________________ ____________________

Wipe It Off

an american woman, mary anderson, had a good idea in 1903. “aha!” she thought. “if you push a rubber blade across a windshield, you can wipe away rain and snow.” what do we call her invention today?

Answer: ______________________________

Name ______________________

Plurals 1

A **plural noun** names more than one thing. Most plurals are formed by adding *s* to the word. But some nouns form their plurals in different ways.

- The plurals of nouns ending in ***sh, ch, x, s,*** or ***z*** are made by adding *es* to the singular.
  brush → brushes fox → foxes glass → glasses
- The plurals of nouns that end in ***y*** with a consonant just before the ***y*** are formed by changing the ***y*** to ***i*** and adding ***es.***
  baby → babies fly → flies
- The plurals of nouns that end in ***y*** with a vowel just before the ***y*** are formed by adding only an ***s.***
  day → days monkey → monkeys

Write the plural form for each singular noun. The first two have been done for you.

1. boss bosses

2. rabbit rabbits

3. mess ______________

4. dish ______________

5. fox ______________

6. ant ______________

7. army ______________

8. plane ______________

9. sky ______________

10. donkey ______________

11. switch ______________

12. buzz ______________

2

Write the correct plurals in the blanks. The first sentence has been done for you.

1. Long ago twin princesses lived in a palace.
   (princess)

2. One night two old ______________ came to the gate.
   (lady)

3. Each lady carried a pile of ______________ .
   (box)

4. "Each box holds three ______________ ," they said.
   (wish)

5. The young ______________ opened the gate.
   (princess)

Next Step **Write a short ending to the story started above.**

Name ______________________________

Plurals 2

A **plural noun** names more than one thing. In this activity, you will practice forming many different plural nouns. (You may use a dictionary with this activity.)

1

Write the plural form for each word listed below.

1. bunch ______________

2. box ______________

3. pitch ______________

4. day ______________

5. story ______________

6. daddy ______________

7. beach ______________

8. glass ______________

9. guess ______________

10. flash ______________

11. jelly ______________

12. key ______________

13. candy ______________

14. baby ______________

2

Write the plural form for each irregular noun below.

1. wolf ______________

2. knife ______________

3. mouse ______________

4. man ______________

5. foot ______________

6. child ______________

Next Step **Write the plural of each word below. Then write a sentence using the plural form of the word.**

1. *singular:* bush *plural:* ____________________

sentence: ____________________

____

2. *singular:* nurse *plural:* ____________________

sentence: ____________________

____

3. *singular:* woman *plural:* ____________________

sentence: ____________________

____

4. *singular:* goose *plural:* ____________________

sentence: ____________________

____

5. *singular:* giant *plural:* ____________________

sentence: ____________________

____

Next Step **Use singular and plural nouns to tell a partner what you would like to find in a treasure chest.**

Name ______________________

Write Source Link

Writing Numbers

- Numbers from one to nine are usually written as words.

  Babe Didrikson Zaharias won five Olympic medals in one year.

- Numbers larger than nine are usually written as numerals.

  The United States won 37 medals at the 2010 Winter Olympics.

TIP: A number at the beginning of a sentence is written as a word.

Follow the directions for each sentence. Write your numbers correctly and be sure to use your *Write Source* book.

1. Write a sentence telling how old you are.

____

2. Write a sentence using a very large number.

____

3. Write a sentence about the number of doors in your classroom.

____

4. Write a sentence naming an amount of money.

____

5. Write a sentence telling how many students are wearing tennis shoes in your class.

____

Name

Using Abbreviations

An **abbreviation** is the shortened form of a word or phrase. Many abbreviations begin with a capital letter and end with a period.

Mister = Mr.
Doctor = Dr.
Street = St.

1 **Circle the abbreviations in this address:**

Mr. Michael Carlson, Jr.
222 W. Bridge Ave.
Greenville, NY 01209

TIP: Postal abbreviations for states have two capital letters and no period.

Massachusetts → MA

Next Step **Write your name and address here. Use at least two abbreviations.**

(Name)

(Street)

(City, State, ZIP)

Name ________________________________

State Abbreviations

Each state has a postal abbreviation that has two letters.

Alabama = AL Minnesota = MN
Wyoming = WY Maine = ME

After each set of clues, write the full name of the state. Then write the two-letter abbreviation for the state. The first one has been done for you.

1. Statue of Liberty, Empire State Building, Niagara Falls New York NY
2. Sunshine State, Kennedy Space Center, Everglades ____________ ______
3. Lone Star State, Alamo, Dallas ____________ ______
4. San Francisco, redwoods, the gold rush ____________ ______
5. St. Louis, Gateway Arch, Lake of the Ozarks ____________ ______
6. Phoenix, Grand Canyon, desert ____________ ______
7. Chicago, Abe Lincoln, Lake Michigan ____________ ______
8. Atlanta, Peach State, Civil War ____________ ______
9. Islands, volcanoes, 50th state ____________ ______
10. Santa Fe, astronomy, Carlsbad Caverns ____________ ______

2 **Make your best guess to answer each question below. Then see *Write Source* pages 498 and 499 to check and correct your work.**

Which is the . . .	State Name	Abbreviation
1. largest state?	________	________
2. smallest state?	________	________
3. state with the highest point? *(northernmost state)*	________	________
4. state with the rainiest spot? *(group of islands)*	________	________
5. state with the driest desert? *(third-largest state)*	________	________

Next Step **Draw a map of your state. Show the state capital, the city or town you live in, and other interesting places. Label your map with the state's name and its postal abbreviation.**

Name ______________________________

Write Source Link
486–499

Mechanics Review

This activity is a review of capitalization, plurals, numbers, and abbreviations.

1 **Fill in the blanks in the sentences below. Make sure to use capital letters and numbers correctly.**

1. ______________________ is a state I want to visit.

2. ______________________ is my favorite holiday, and ______________________ is my favorite month.

3. The abbreviation of my favorite month is ______________.

4. There are ______________ students in my class.

5. Many third graders are ______________ years old.

6. One of my textbooks is called ______________________, and I am on chapter ______________.

7. My handbook is called ______________________, and one chapter is called "______________________."

8. There are ______________ pages in *Write Source.*

2 Rewrite the addresses below, using as many abbreviations as you can.

Doctor Lee Strong ____________________

142 South Jefferson Drive ____________________

River City, Wisconsin 54999 ____________________

Mister Charles Johnson, Junior ____________________

3730 Azalea Street West ____________________

Wellington, South Carolina 29777 ____________________

3 Write the plural form of each word below. Write it under the rule that explains how to make it plural. The first one has been done for you.

bee	cow	lady	crunch	splash
cook	kitty	mess	kite	fly

1. Plurals of most nouns are made by adding an *s*.

bees ____________________ ____________________

____________________ ____________________

2. If a noun ends in *sh, ch, x, s,* or *z,* make the plural by adding *es*.

____________ ____________ ____________

3. If a noun ends in *y* with a consonant just before the *y*, change the *y* to *i* and add *es*.

____________ ____________ ____________

Name ______________________________

Spelling and Alphabetizing

Write Source Link

503

1 **Rewrite the list of birds, putting them in alphabetical (ABC) order.**

robin	**cardinal**	**eagle**
seagull	**penguin**	**hawk**
falcon	**ostrich**	**loon**
albatross	**wren**	**tern**
bluebird	**vulture**	**duck**

1. ______________________

2. ______________________

3. ______________________

4. ______________________

5. ______________________

6. ______________________

7. ______________________

8. ______________________

9. ______________________

10. ______________________

11. ______________________

12. ______________________

13. ______________________

14. ______________________

15. ______________________

2 Write the words in alphabetical (ABC) order. When words begin with the same letter, be sure to look at the second and third letters of the words.

1. drive, dressed, dumb

____

____

____

2. toward, truth, tonight

____

____

____

3. might, middle, minute

____

____

____

4. bright, bunch, built

____

____

____

5. planet, picture, phone

____

____

____

6. pencil, past, person

____

____

____

Name ______________________________

Spelling and Silent Letters

1 Choose a word from the list to fill in each blank below. After you write the word, circle the silent consonant or consonants. The first one has been done for you.

autumn	**island**	**night**
calf	**knee**	**rhyme**
castle	**lamb**	**write**
gnat	**listen**	

1. The sun shines by day and the moon by ______night______.
2. A baby sheep is called a ______________________.
3. When your teacher is talking, it's important to ______________________.
4. Another name for fall is ______________________.
5. A king and a queen are sure to live in a ______________________.
6. A baby cow is called a ______________________.
7. Poems and songs often have words that ______________________.
8. A ______________________ is a tiny bug.
9. It's fun to ______________________ letters to friends far away.
10. Your leg bends at the ______________________.
11. An ______________________ is a piece of land surrounded by water.

2 Sort the words below into three groups: one-syllable words, two-syllable words, and three-syllable words.

answer	Friday	knife	right
bought	ghost	middle	science
different	happiness	neighbor	special
dressed	hurry	often	weather
dumb	interest	president	whole
finally	kitchen	probably	would

One-Syllable Words

1. ______________________ 5. ______________________

2. ______________________ 6. ______________________

3. ______________________ 7. ______________________

4. ______________________ 8. ______________________

Two-Syllable Words

1. ______________________ 6. ______________________

2. ______________________ 7. ______________________

3. ______________________ 8. ______________________

4. ______________________ 9. ______________________

5. ______________________ 10. ______________________

Three-Syllable Words

1. ______________________ 4. ______________________

2. ______________________ 5. ______________________

3. ______________________ 6. ______________________

Name ______________________________

Spelling Sorts

1 Sort the words below into two groups. First list all the words that have double consonants. Then list all the words that have silent consonants.

answer	finally	mirror	tonight
bought	ghost	often	worry
different	guess	really	wrong
dressed	hurry	right	
dumb	knife	science	

Words with Double Consonants

1. ______________ 5. ______________
2. ______________ 6. ______________
3. ______________ 7. ______________
4. ______________ 8. ______________

Words with Silent Consonants

1. ______________ 6. ______________
2. ______________ 7. ______________
3. ______________ 8. ______________
4. ______________ 9. ______________
5. ______________ 10. ______________

2 **Using the spelling words on pages 503, 504, and 506 in *Write Source,* write the answers to these riddles.**

1. The first meal of the day ______________________
2. The United States ______________________
3. The opposite of awake ______________________
4. Sounds the same as the word "right" ______________________
5. The opposite of picked up ______________________
6. 10 X 0 equals . . . ______________________
7. Land surrounded by water ______________________
8. The first month of the year ______________________
9. The last month of the year ______________________
10. The day after today ______________________
11. One of three blind mice ______________________
12. The opposite of wrong ______________________
13. A synonym for "fast" ______________________
14. A writer of books ______________________
15. The plural of "child" ______________________

Next Step **Using the words from the list, write a short story that could make someone laugh.**

Name ________________________________

Using the Right Word 1

Homophones are words that sound the same but have different spellings and meanings. Let's look at two sets of homophones.

I **ate** a sandwich.

Eight players were sick yesterday.

The grizzly **bear** is a big animal.

There is a **bare** spot on the lawn.

1

Write the correct word in each blank.

1. Jermaine says he likes to watch the old polar __________ at the zoo.
2. Yesterday, the polar __________ __________ three huge fish.
3. He counted __________ blue jays trying to get the scraps.
4. The polar __________ found a __________ spot in the grass to lie down after dinner.

Next Step **Write one sentence using each of these words: *bear, bare, ate,* and *eight.***

____

____

____

____

____

Name ______________________

Write Source Link
512

Using the Right Word 2

Homophones are words that sound alike but have different spellings and different meanings.

Don't **break** the glass.

The bike's front **brake** is loose.

Joe likes to swim in the **creek**.

There is a **creak** in the wooden floor.

1 **Write the correct word from the list in each blank.**

break **brake** **creek** **creak**

1. Jamie caught a big fish in the ____________.
2. At first, he thought the fish would ____________ his fishing line.
3. He set the ____________ on the fishing reel.
4. Suddenly, he heard his old fishing rod ____________.
5. When Jamie lifted the fish out of the water, he was sure it was the biggest fish in the ____________.

Next Step **In a few sentences, write a little story that uses these four words: *break, brake, creek,* and *creak.***

Name ______________________________

Using the Right Word 3

Homophones are words that sound alike but have different spellings and meanings.

The **hole** in the gound is deep.

She bought the **whole** set of books.

I **hear** a rooster crowing.

Bill is **here** today.

1 Write the correct word in each blank.

hole **whole** **hear** **here**

1. Liu's mom said, "I ____________ it's going to rain all day."
2. Liu brought out a board game that the ____________ family could play.
3. He pulled the box off the shelf in his room and was surprised to see that it had a big ____________.
4. All of a sudden the box lid moved, and he could ____________ something inside the box.
5. He lifted the lid and saw that his hamster had chewed up a ____________ set of score sheets.
6. "How did the hamster get ____________ from his cage?" he wondered.

Name ______________________________

Write Source Link
516

Using the Right Word 4

Homophones are words that sound alike but have different spellings and meanings. Let's look at two sets of common homophones: *its, it's* and *meat, meet.*

It's vacation time.

Our school needs its summer "checkup."

(*It's* stands for it is; *its* shows ownership.)

Some people don't eat red meat

At recess, I will meet you by the swings.

1 Write the correct word—*it's* or *its*—in each blank.

1. Our gym needs ____________ clock fixed.
2. ____________ always slow.
3. We never know when ____________ time to go back to our classroom.
4. Our gym needs ____________ water fountain checked, too.

2 Write the correct word—*meat* or *meet*—in each blank.

1. Some restaurants use the best ____________ to make hamburger.
2. Jolene plans to ____________ Cari at the library.
3. Will you ____________ me in the lunchroom?
4. What kind of ____________ do you put in chili?

Name ______________________________

Using the Right Word 5

Homophones are words that sound alike but have different spellings and meanings.

A **pear** is a tasty fruit.

Franklin put on his brown **pair** of socks.

Jill's mother will **pare** the carrots for stew.

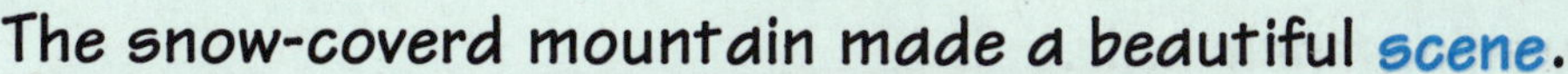

The snow-coverd mountain made a beautiful **scene**.

Have you **seen** my school books?

1 Use *pear, pair,* or *pare* to fill in the blanks.

1. Will someone ____________ the apples for me?
2. The camp said I should bring a ____________ of hiking boots.
3. The ____________ is still too green to eat.
4. This ____________ of pictures will fit on this wall.

2 Write *scene* or *seen* to fill in the blanks.

1. I have ____________ that movie at least three times.
2. The heavy rain hid the hilly ____________ below the cabin.
3. Jan has ____________ this display already.

Next Step **Write a sentence for each of the following words: *pair* and *seen*.**

Name ______________________________

Write Source Link

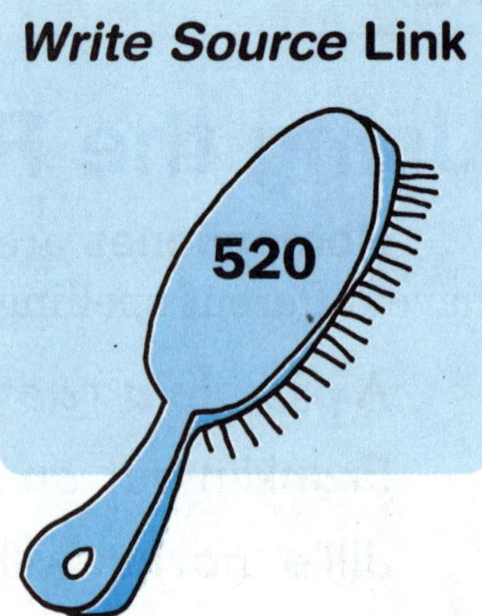

Using the Right Word 6

Homophones are words that sound the same but have different spellings and meanings. Let's look at five common homophones: *there, their, they're* and *tail, tale.*

I put my hairbrush **there**.

The girls need **their** hairbrushes.

They're brushing their hair.

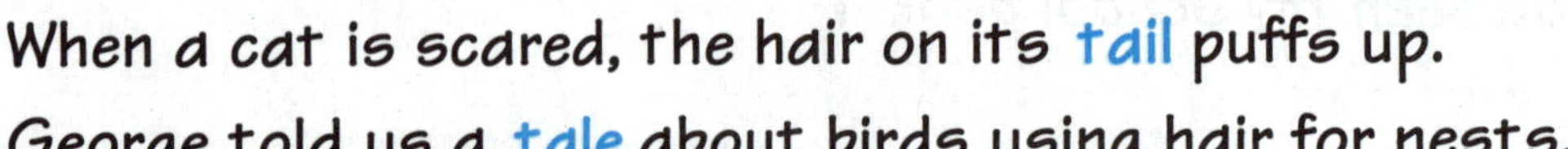

When a cat is scared, the hair on its **tail** puffs up.

George told us a **tale** about birds using hair for nests.

1

Write the correct word—*there, their, they're* and *tail* or *tale*—in each blank.

1. ____________ are about 100,000 hairs on your head.
2. Rapunzel is a ____________ about a woman with very long hair.
3. ____________ always falling out—from 25-125 hairs a day.
4. ____________ are many kinds of hair.
5. Many people wish ____________ hair was curly.
6. Some men lose ____________ hair and become bald.
7. Some hairdos are named after the ____________ of a pony or a pig.
8. Tell me a ____________ about a woman with bright green hair.

Next Step **Write a sentence for each of the following words: *there, they're,* and *tale.***

Name ______________________________

Using the Right Word 7

Homophones are words that sound alike but have different spellings and different meanings. Let's look at some common homophones: *two, to, too* and *your, you're.*

For two years, Harry went to the chili contest.

Matilda went, too.

The chili was too hot for Harry.

Is this your bowl of chili?

You're supposed to eat the chili now.

1 **Write the correct word—*too, two, to, your,* or *you're*—in each blank.**

1. This year, Matilda wanted __________ go to the chili contest.
2. She said to Harry, "I hope __________ going to go with me."
3. He said, "I have already been there __________ times."
4. He thought three times would be __________ much.
5. He wanted __________ see the frog-jumping contest instead.
6. He said to Matilda, "__________ welcome to come with me."
7. Matilda said, "It would be fun if __________ of us go."
8. She told Harry, "__________ frog contest was fun, but I'm hungry."
9. So then they went __________ the chili contest.

Name ______________________

Write Source Link
510–523

Using the Right Word Review

1 **If the underlined homophone in each sentence is used incorrectly, cross it out and write the correct word above it. The first one has been done for you.**

1. I have ~~ate~~ eight shoelaces.
2. Jon saw a bare at the wildlife park.
3. Be careful not to break that glass bowl.
4. Because of the heavy rain, the creak is flooding.
5. I think its going to rain all night.
6. I gave my mom a new pair of slippers for her birthday.
7. Have you seen the new movie about Sammy the Seal?
8. Did you here about our field trip to the orange-juice factory?
9. Bob's cat ate a hole bowl of tuna salad that was on the counter.
10. Billy has too buckets to make sand castles at the beach.
11. Do you have you're ticket for the movie?
12. That squirrel has a very stubby tail.
13. There are several empty boxes in the hallway.

2

Sentence Activities

This section includes activities related to basic sentence writing, kinds of sentences, sentence problems, and sentence combining. The Next Step activities often require original writing.

Sentence Basics	**77**
Sentence Problems	**93**
Sentence Combining	**101**

Name ________________________________

Write Source Link
400, 526, 528

Simple and Complete Subjects and Predicates

The **complete subject** of a sentence names someone or something. The **simple subject** is the main word in the complete subject.

The **complete predicate** (verb) tells what the subject is or does. The **simple predicate** is the main word in the complete predicate.

1 **Fill in each blank with a simple or complete subject that makes sense. Underline the simple subjects once.**

1. ______________________ takes piano lessons.

2. ______________________ walks to school.

3. ______________________ wag their tails when they are happy.

4. ______________________ stampeded across the prairie.

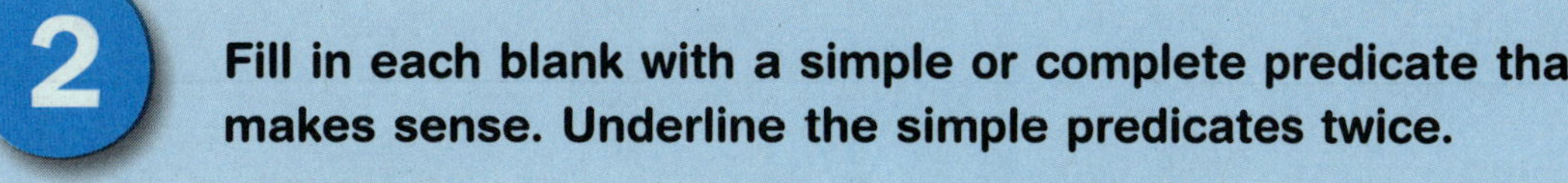

2 **Fill in each blank with a simple or complete predicate that makes sense. Underline the simple predicates twice.**

1. Ryan ______________________.

2. The teacher ______________________.

3. The sun ______________________.

4. Susie ______________________.

In each sentence below, underline the simple subject once and underline the simple predicate twice.

1. Diana plays first base.
2. The thunder scared Timmy.
3. Schuyler lives next door.
4. Pizza is my favorite food.
5. Maria won.
6. Peter did the dishes.
7. Summer is the best time of year.

Next Step Think of three people you know. Tell a partner one sentence about something each person is or does. Each sentence should contain a complete subject and a complete predicate. Then write your sentences. Underline the simple subject of each sentence once and the simple predicate twice.

1. ______________________________

____

2. ______________________________

____

3. ______________________________

Name ____________________

Subject of a Sentence

- Every sentence has a subject and a predicate. The **complete subject** of a sentence names something or someone.

  My old friend jumped over the candlestick.

  (*My old friend* is the complete subject.)

- The **simple subject** is the main word in the subject.

  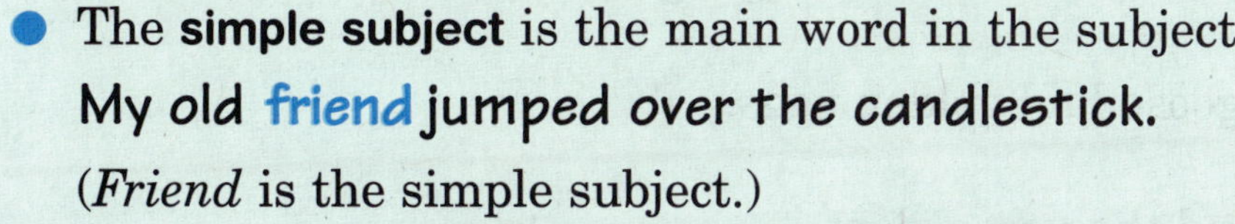

  My old friend jumped over the candlestick.

  (*Friend* is the simple subject.)

- A **compound subject** is made up of two or more simple subjects.

  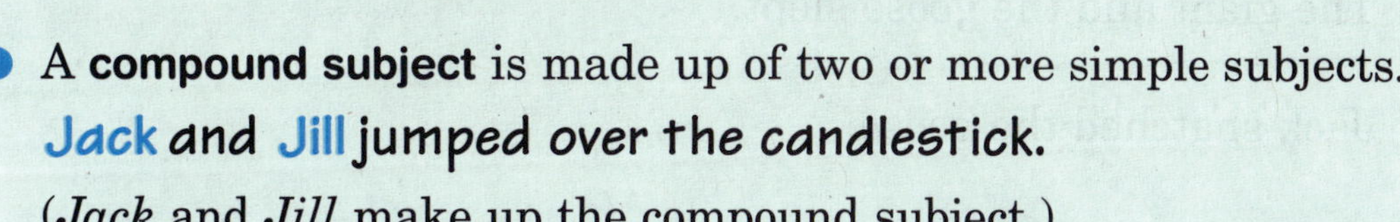

  Jack and Jill jumped over the candlestick.

  (*Jack* and *Jill* make up the compound subject.)

Draw a line under each complete subject. Circle each simple subject. The first one has been done for you.

1. A few little seeds fell to the ground.
2. An enormous beanstalk grew up and up.
3. Brave Jack climbed the beanstalk.
4. A huge castle rose up out of the clouds.
5. The ugly giant roared, "Fee, fie, fo, fum!"
6. The giant's wife saved Jack.
7. An old clock protected Jack from the giant.
8. Frightened little Jack stayed very still.

2 **Draw a line under the complete subject in each sentence below. Write an *S* in the blank if the main part of the subject is simple or a *C* if the main part is compound. The first one has been done for you.**

C **1.** The giant and his wife ate dinner.

_____ **2.** The ugly giant called for his magic goose.

_____ **3.** The magic goose laid golden eggs.

_____ **4.** The giant and the goose slept.

_____ **5.** Jack snatched the goose.

_____ **6.** The bold boy climbed down the beanstalk.

_____ **7.** The surprised giant chased him.

_____ **8.** Jack's mother chopped down the beanstalk.

_____ **9.** Jack and his mother lived happily ever after.

Next Step **Tell your partner three sentences about a favorite fairy tale. Write the complete subject for each sentence you say.**

1. *complete subject:* ____________________

2. *complete subject:* ____________________

3. *complete subject:* ____________________

Name ______________________________

Predicate of a Sentence

- Remember, every sentence has a subject and a predicate. The **complete predicate** of a sentence tells what something or someone is or does.

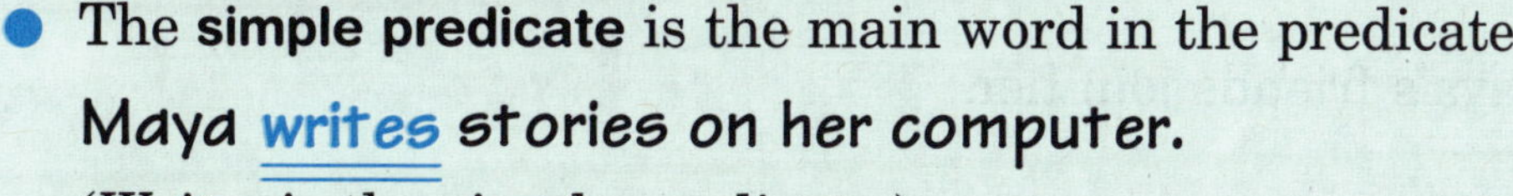

(*Writes stories on her computer* is the complete predicate.)

- The **simple predicate** is the main word in the predicate.

Maya writes stories on her computer.

(*Writes* is the simple predicate.)

- A **compound predicate** is made up of two or more simple predicates.

Maya writes stories and plays music on her computer.

(*Writes* and *plays* make up the compound predicate.)

Draw two lines under each complete predicate. Circle each simple predicate, or verb. The first one has been done for you.

1. Maya thinks of good stories.
2. Maya writes about a magic keyboard.
3. The keyboard creates 100-page stories overnight.
4. Everybody loves the stories.
5. She wins dozens of prizes.
6. She becomes a great author.
7. Maya wants a magic keyboard like this.

2

Draw two lines under the complete predicate in each sentence below. Write an *S* in the blank if the main part of the predicate is simple. Write a *C* if the main part of the predicate is compound.

C **1.** Maya sings and composes music.

_____ **2.** Maya composes music on her computer.

_____ **3.** She plays the melody and sings the words.

_____ **4.** Maya's friends join her.

_____ **5.** They sing old songs and make up new ones.

_____ **6.** Maya's dog sings, too.

_____ **7.** The dog barks and howls.

_____ **8.** Maya's mother listens to the singing.

_____ **9.** She smiles and shakes her head.

_____ **10.** She joins in the fun.

_____ **11.** Everyone has a good time.

Next Step **Tell a partner a sentence about the best computer game. Write the complete predicate for the sentence. Repeat with a sentence about you and your friends.**

1. *complete predicate:* ______________________________

2. *complete predicate:* ______________________________

Name ___________________________

Write Source Link
398–401, 526, 528

Subject and Predicate Review

In these sentences, underline each complete subject once and underline the complete predicate twice. The first one has been done for you.

1. Betty Bodette drives a red convertible.
2. My father drives a truck.
3. The truck belongs to a landscaping company.
4. I ride with my father sometimes.
5. My big sister comes, too.
6. We help my father.
7. He treats us to lunch at noon.

2

Put a check in the subject box if the sentence has a compound subject. Put a check in the predicate box if the sentence has a compound predicate.

	COMPOUND	
	Subject	Predicate
1. Betty and her sister drive to the mall.	✔	
2. Betty buys a sundae and goes to the movies.		
3. Betty and her sister like funny movies.		
4. Her brother skateboards and plays video games.		
5. He and his friends like to ride in the convertible.		

3

Write four sentences about a vacation you would like to go on. Underline the complete subject in each sentence once. Underline the complete predicate in each sentence twice.

1. ______________________________

____

2. ______________________________

____

3. ______________________________

____

4. ______________________________

____

4

Discuss with a partner what you would need to pack for your dream vacation. Then write two complete subjects and two complete predicates that you said.

1. *complete subject:* ______________________

2. *complete predicate:* ______________________

3. *complete subject:* ______________________

4. *complete predicate:* ______________________

Name ______________________________

Simple and Compound Sentences 1

- A **simple sentence** has one main thought.

  You have two eyes.

- A **compound sentence** is two simple sentences joined by a comma and a connecting word (such as *and, but,* or *so*).

  You have two eyes, and they both see the same thing.

1 **Carefully read the following sentences. Write an *S* in the blank for each simple sentence and a *C* for each compound sentence. The first two have been done for you.**

__S__ **1.** Miss Filbert loves science.

__C__ **2.** She talked about eyesight, and then she did an experiment.

_____ **3.** Miss Filbert threw a ball to Peter, and he threw it back to her.

_____ **4.** She caught the ball.

_____ **5.** Then she put on an eye patch.

_____ **6.** Peter threw the ball again.

_____ **7.** Miss Filbert reached out to catch the ball, but she missed it.

_____ **8.** Miss Filbert made an important point.

_____ **9.** Two eyes help us see in 3-D, and they help us catch a ball.

2 **Combine each set of simple sentences to make a compound sentence. The first one has been done for you.**

1. Some eyes are blue. Some eyes are brown.

   Some eyes are blue, and some eyes are brown.

2. A horse has two eyes. They are on the sides of its head.

3. A human has simple eyes. A dragonfly has compound eyes.

4. Fish see underwater. Many of them see in color.

Next Step **Write one simple sentence and one compound sentence about your eyes.**

Simple Sentence:

Compound Sentence:

Name ______________________________

Write Source Link

410

Simple and Compound Sentences 2

- A **simple sentence** has one main thought. (Although it may have two subjects or two verbs.)

Jerry wrote a poem.

(This simple sentence has one subject and one verb.)

Jerry and Talia wrote a poem.

(This simple sentence has two subjects and one verb.)

Jerry wrote a poem and drew a picture.

(This simple sentence has one subject and two verbs.)

- A **compound sentence** is two simple sentences joined by a comma and a connecting word.

Jerry and Talia wrote a poem, and I read it.

(This compound sentence expresses two thoughts.)

1 **Carefully read each sentence. Write an *S* in the blank for each simple sentence and a *C* for each compound sentence. (*Hint:* A compound sentence must have a comma and a connecting word such as *and, or, but,* or *so.*)**

_____ **1.** Marisa and Tom read the same book.

_____ **2.** Charlie drew a picture and gave it to me.

_____ **3.** I cleaned the hamster cage, and Anthony watered the plants.

_____ **4.** The teacher and parents had a meeting.

_____ **5.** Brittany forgot her sweater, so I loaned her mine.

_____ **6.** It started to rain, and we closed the windows.

2 Write the following types of sentences about things that have happened in your classroom.

1. Write a simple sentence with one subject and one predicate (verb).

____

____

2. Write a simple sentence with two subjects and one verb. (Your sentence will be about two people who did one thing.)

____

____

3. Write a compound sentence. (Your sentence will be two simple sentences joined with a comma and a connecting word.)

____

____

4. Write one more compound sentence about your class.

____

____

Next Step **Trade papers with a partner. Read and check each other's sentences. Make sure you followed directions correctly.**

Name ______________________________

Write Source Link

Simple Sentences and Subject-Verb Agreement

A **simple sentence** has one subject and one verb. The **subject** and the **verb** must agree in number.

A **singular** subject must have a singular verb.

I am good at playing basketball.

subject verb

A **plural** subject must have a plural verb.

My friends are good at playing basketball, too.

subject verb

1 Write the correct word—*live* or *lives*—in each blank.

1. I ____________ in Houston now.
2. My friend ____________ in Houston near me.
3. I used to ____________ in San Antonio.
4. My old friend still ____________ in San Antonio.

2 Write the correct word—*am, are*, or *is*—in each blank.

1. I ____________ good at checkers.
2. You ____________ are great at running races.
3. She ____________ the fastest swimmer of all.
4. They ____________ learning soccer at camp.

2 Rewrite each sentence so that the subject and verb agree in number.

1. Enchiladas is my favorite food of all time.

____

____

2. Spaghetti and lasagna has the best flavor of any Italian food.

____

____

3. Most people loves cake and ice cream at a party.

____

____

4. Chocolate make any dessert delicious.

____

____

5. Fruits and vegetables is probably the healthiest foods.

____

____

Next Step **Tell a partner about your favorite restaurant. Use simple sentences with correct subject-verb agreement. Have your partner to identify the subjects and verbs.**

Name ______________________________

Write Source Link
388, 406

Compound Sentences and Subject-Verb Agreement

A **compound sentence** has two or more simple sentences joined by a comma and a **conjunction** *(and, but, or)*.

Each **subject** and **verb** pair must agree in number. A **singular** subject must have a singular verb. A **plural** subject must have a plural verb.

Melinda goes to the dog park, but Peter and Carol go to the jogging trail.

subject verb subject verb

1 Write the correct word—*go* or *goes*—in each blank.

1. Every summer I ______________ to a camp on a lake, and Brian ______________ to a camp in the woods.

2. I ______________ fishing in the lake, but Brian ______________ hiking in the woods.

2 Write the correct word—*have* or *has*—in each blank.

1. I ______________ two dogs for pets, and Ben ______________ four cats.

2. My dogs ______________ fancy colors, and Ben's cats ______________ plain collars.

3. Sacha ______________ a snake, but snakes don't ______________ collars!

3 Choose the correct word from each pair, and write it in the blank.

I __________ (has, have) a great brother, and he __________ (is, are) my twin. Having a brother __________ (is, are) great, but having a best friend for a brother __________ (is, are) fantastic. We __________ (look, looks) a lot alike, but Max __________ (is, are) different from me in some ways, too. I __________ (has, have) blue eyes, but Max __________ (has, have) brown eyes. I __________ (am, is) quite tall for my age, and Max __________ (am, is) even taller than me. I __________ (wear, wears) jeans a lot, but Max __________ (wear, wears) shorts all the time!

4 Tell a partner three compound sentences about a game you play with a friend. Use correct subject-verb agreement. Have your partner identify the subjects and verbs that you use.

Name ________________________________

Sentence Fragments 1

A complete sentence has a subject and a predicate. If either one or both of these are missing, you have a **sentence fragment**.

- In this sentence fragment, the subject is missing.

Fragment: Jumped off the diving board.

Corrected Sentence: Jeb jumped off the diving board. (A subject has been added.)

- In this sentence fragment, the subject and verb are missing.

Fragment: In the pool.

Corrected Sentence: Jenna and Jane swam in the pool. (A subject and verb have been added.)

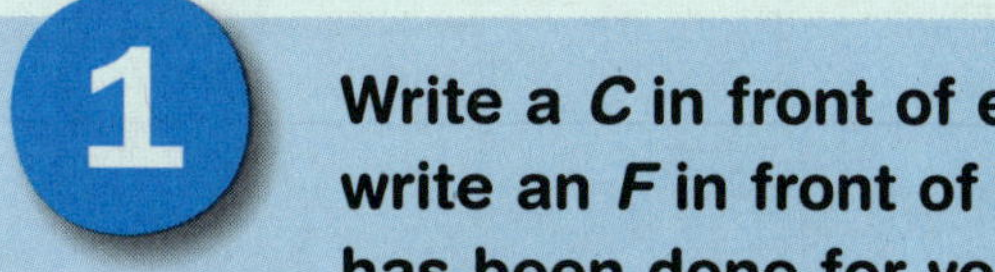

1 **Write a *C* in front of each complete sentence below, and write an *F* in front of each sentence fragment. The first one has been done for you.**

__F__ **1.** An excellent swimmer.

_____ **2.** Herman is an excellent swimmer.

_____ **3.** Breaststroke, Australian crawl, and backstroke.

_____ **4.** He is teaching me how to swim.

_____ **5.** I am leaving.

_____ **6.** Because of the weather.

2 Correct each sentence fragment below.

1. In the ocean.

   Missy McGee swims in the ocean.

2. Bought scuba equipment.

3. Below the surface.

4. Colorful fish everywhere.

5. Because of the sharks.

6. Reached the boat.

Next Step Use one of the sentences you wrote to tell a story to a partner. Use complete subjects and complete predicates as you speak.

Name ______________________________

Sentence Fragments 2

Remember, a complete sentence has a complete subject and a complete predicate. The complete subject names who or what the sentence is about. The complete predicate tells what the subject does. If either one or both are missing, you have a **sentence fragment**.

Read the paragraphs below. (If possible, read aloud with a partner.) Then underline each sentence fragment.

Two Orphan Cubs by Erika Kors. A true story about two bear cubs. One day their mother left them forever. Gary Alt found the cubs in the den. Very hungry and lonely. Put the little bears into a sack. Took the bears to Molly's den. Molly was a bear and had two of her own cubs.

A great story. I liked it. Because there was a happy ending.

Rewrite the paragraphs, using complete sentences.

____

____

____

____

____

____

____

____

Name ________________________________

Sentence Fragments 3

When you are using the word *because* in a sentence, make sure you don't end up with a fragment. To make a sentence, the word *because* must be combined with two complete thoughts. After you include the word *because* in your sentence, check that you still have two complete subjects and two complete predicates.

Fragment: Because it had a happy ending.

Corrected Sentence: I liked it *because* it had a happy ending.

1 **Make each sentence fragment below into a complete sentence.**

1. ________________________ because I missed lunch.
2. ________________________ because she is sick.
3. ________________________ because it is my birthday.
4. My friend was late because ________________________.
5. I can't go because ________________________.
6. He's happy because ________________________.

Next Step **Write a complete sentence using the word *because*.**

____

____

Name ______________________

Write Source Link **404**

Run-On Sentences 1

A **run-on sentence** happens when two or more sentences run together.

Run-On Sentence:
Mr. Wiggle's lawn mower needs repair he can't fix it.

Corrected Sentences:
Mr. Wiggle's lawn mower needs repair. He can't fix it.
(two sentences)

Mr. Wiggle's lawn mower needs repair, but he can't fix it.
(compound sentence)

Change each of these run-on sentences into two sentences.

1. He pulled the cord the engine didn't start.

He pulled the cord. The engine didn't start.

2. His grass was growing fast dandelions were popping up.

____

____

3. Mr. Wiggle borrowed our mower he has not returned it yet.

____

____

4. I hope he gives it back soon our grass is getting very long.

____

____

2 **Correct each run-on sentence below by rewriting the run-on as a compound sentence. (See *Write Source* 410.) The first one has been done for you.**

1. Mr. Witt toasted some bread it burned.

Mr. Witt toasted some bread, but it burned.

2. The smoke set off a fire alarm the fire department came.

3. Mr. Witt was surprised to see the firefighters he told them what happened.

4. Mr. Witt threw out the toaster Mrs. Witt pulled it from the trash.

5. Mr. Witt bought a new toaster his wife fixed the old one.

6. Now the Witts have two toasters we're thinking of borrowing one.

Next Step **Pair up with a classmate and check each other's compound sentences. Make sure your partner has placed a comma before the connecting word in each of his or her sentences.**

Name ______________________________

Run-On Sentences 2

A run-on sentence happens when two or more sentences run together.

Run-On Sentence:
We read about Vikings they were smart.

Corrected Sentences:
We read about Vikings. They were smart.

1 Change each run-on sentence into two sentences.

1. The Vikings came to North America before Columbus they were the first Europeans to come here.

____

____

2. Vikings were also called Norsemen northern Europe was their home.

____

____

3. The Vikings were good sailors they were also warriors.

____

____

4. Once Vikings sailed to England their ships sailed up a river to London.

____

____

2 **Correct each run-on sentence by rewriting it as a compound sentence. See *Write Source* page 410.**

1. Eric the Red led Vikings to Greenland his son Leif later led Vikings to Canada.

____

____

2. No one knows why they sailed to Canada there were no towns there to raid.

____

____

3. Some experts think they were fishing a storm blew their ships off course.

____

____

Next Step **Write two run-on sentences about a topic you are studying. Your sentences can be serious or silly. Trade papers with a partner and correct each other's run-ons.**

1. ____

____

2. ____

____

Name ______________________________

Combining Sentences with a Key Word

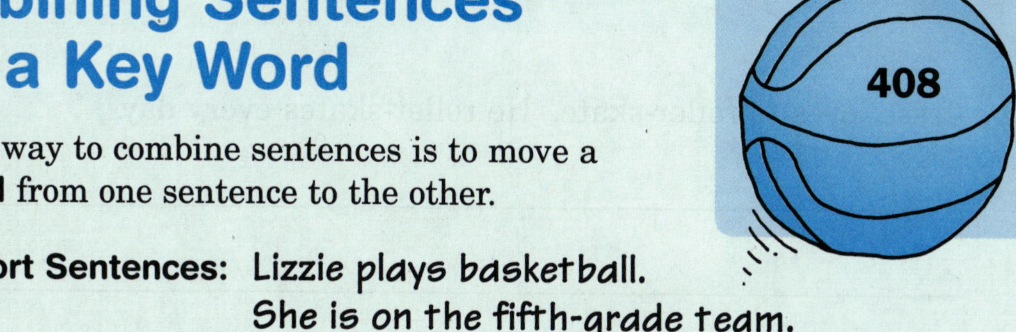

One way to combine sentences is to move a **key word** from one sentence to the other.

Short Sentences: Lizzie plays basketball.
She is on the fifth-grade team.

Combined Sentence: Lizzie plays on the (fifth-grade) basketball team.
(The key word is circled.)

1 **Circle the key word or words that were used to make a combined sentence. The first one has been done for you.**

1. **Short sentences:** Her team has new uniforms.
They are blue and white.
Combined sentence: Her team has new (blue and white) uniforms.

2. **Short sentences:** Ms. Charleyhorse is the coach.
She coaches basketball.
Combined sentence: Ms. Charleyhorse is the basketball coach.

3. **Short sentences:** The team goes to away games in a van.
The van is brand-new.
Combined sentence: The team goes to away games in a brand-new van.

4. **Short sentences:** Laura cheers for Lizzie's team.
She cheers loudly.
Combined sentence: Laura cheers loudly for Lizzie's team.

2 **Combine each set of sentences below by moving a key word or words from one sentence to the other.**

1. Jesse loves to roller-skate. He roller-skates every day.

2. Jesse sometimes uses his brother's roller skates. The roller skates are green.

3. Jesse likes to roller-skate with his friends. He has five friends.

4. His friends are going to roller-skate with him. They will roller-skate tomorrow.

5. Everyone will practice for a race. The race will be long.

Next Step **Write two short sentences about one of your favorite activities. Combine your ideas into one longer sentence. (Use your own paper for your work.)**

Name ______________________________

Combining Sentences with a Series of Words or Phrases 1

You can combine sentences by listing words or phrases in a series. This can be done if the subjects and verbs are the same in the sentences you want to combine. Include commas between each word or phrase in the series.

Short Sentences: I like camping. I like hiking. I like swimming.

Combined Sentence: I like camping, hiking, and swimming.

1 **Fill in the blanks to complete each group of short sentences. Then combine each group to make one longer sentence.**

1. I like to play ______________________________.

I like to play ______________________________.

I like to play ______________________________.

Combined sentence: ______________________________

____

2. I like to read ______________________________.

I like to read ______________________________.

I like to read ______________________________.

Combined sentence: ______________________________

2 **In the space below, draw a picture of a make-believe animal. Then use words in a series to write sentences about your animal.**

1. Write a sentence telling three things your animal likes to eat.

____

____

2. Write a sentence telling three places your animal likes to hide.

____

____

3. Write a sentence telling three things your animal can do.

____

____

Name ______________________________

Combining Sentences with a Series of Words or Phrases 2

You can combine short sentences that tell different things about the same subject. Remember, use commas between words or phrases in a series.

Short Sentences: *George Washington Carver was curious. He was smart. He was hardworking.*

Combined Sentence: *George Washington Carver was curious, smart, and hardworking.* (The three words in a series tell different things about the subject.)

1 **Combine these sentences using a series of words or phrases.**

1. As a boy, George Washington Carver worked as a cook. He worked as a launderer. He worked as a janitor.

____

____

2. In the laboratory, Carver found new ways to use peanuts. He found new ways to use pecans. He found new ways to use sweet potatoes.

____

____

3. Carver made ink from sweet potatoes. He made flour from sweet potatoes. He made rubber from sweet potatoes.

____

____

2 **Combine these sentences by using a key word from one sentence or by using words or phrases in a series.**

1. Thomas Edison invented a lightbulb. He invented a phonograph. He invented a movie camera.

___

___

2. Edison asked questions that began with "why." He asked questions that began with "how."

___

___

3. Edison's inventions were easy to use. They were easy to keep in order. They were easy to fix.

___

___

4. He worked long hours and took only naps. The naps were short.

___

Next Step **Thomas Edison made improvements in many modern inventions, including batteries, typewriters, microphones, telephones, and radios. Write a sentence naming three of the things he helped to improve.**

___

___

___

Name ______________________

Write Source Link

401, 409

Combining Sentences with Compound Subjects and Verbs 1

Short Sentences: LaJoy went to the circus.
Kelly went to the circus.

Combined Sentence: LaJoy and Kelly went to the circus.
(*LaJoy* and *Kelly* make up a compound subject.)

* * * * * * * * *

Short Sentences: LaJoy went to the circus.
She watched the clowns.

Combined Sentence: LaJoy went to the circus and watched the clowns.
(*Went* and *watched* make up a compound verb.)

Draw lines under the compound subject or the compound verb in each combined sentence.

1. **Short sentences:** Tim likes the trapeze artists.
Henry likes the trapeze artists.
Combined sentence: Tim and Henry like the trapeze artists.

2. **Short sentences:** High-wire performers ride bikes.
They walk on their hands.
Combined sentence: High-wire performers ride bikes and walk on their hands.

3. **Short sentences:** Aerialists hang by their teeth.
They twirl around.
Combined sentence: Aerialists hang by their teeth and twirl around.

2 Combine each pair of sentences using a compound subject or a compound verb.

1. Kelly munched popcorn. She gobbled peanuts.

2. Hector wanted cotton candy. His brother wanted cotton candy, too.

3. LaJoy bought balloons. Tim also bought balloons.

4. Kelly bought a clown wig. She stuck it on her head.

Next Step **Write two sentences about a circus. In one sentence, use a compound subject. In the other sentence, use a compound verb.**

Compound Subject: ______

Compound Verb: ______

Name ______________________________

Combining Sentences with Compound Subjects and Verbs 2

Here's more practice using compound subjects and verbs to combine sentences.

Combine each group of sentences using a compound subject or verb. The first one has been done for you.

1. Once a hen lived on a farm. A cat also lived on the farm. A pig also lived on the farm.

   Once a hen, a cat, and a pig lived on a farm.

2. The hen gathered some wheat. The hen ground some wheat.

   ____

3. The cat refused to help her. The pig refused to help her, too.

   ____

4. The hen baked two loaves of bread. The hen ate two loaves of bread.

   ____

5. The cat begged for some bread. The pig begged for some, too.

   ____

2

Write two sentences about the animals in the sentences on page 109. Use compound subjects in both of your sentences. Then write two more sentences about the animals, using compound verbs.

Sentences with compound subjects:

1. ______________________________

____

2. ______________________________

____

Sentences with compound verbs:

1. ______________________________

____

2. ______________________________

____

Next Step **Draw a picture about one of your sentences.**

Name ___________________________

Sentence Combining Review 1

Write Source Link
408–410

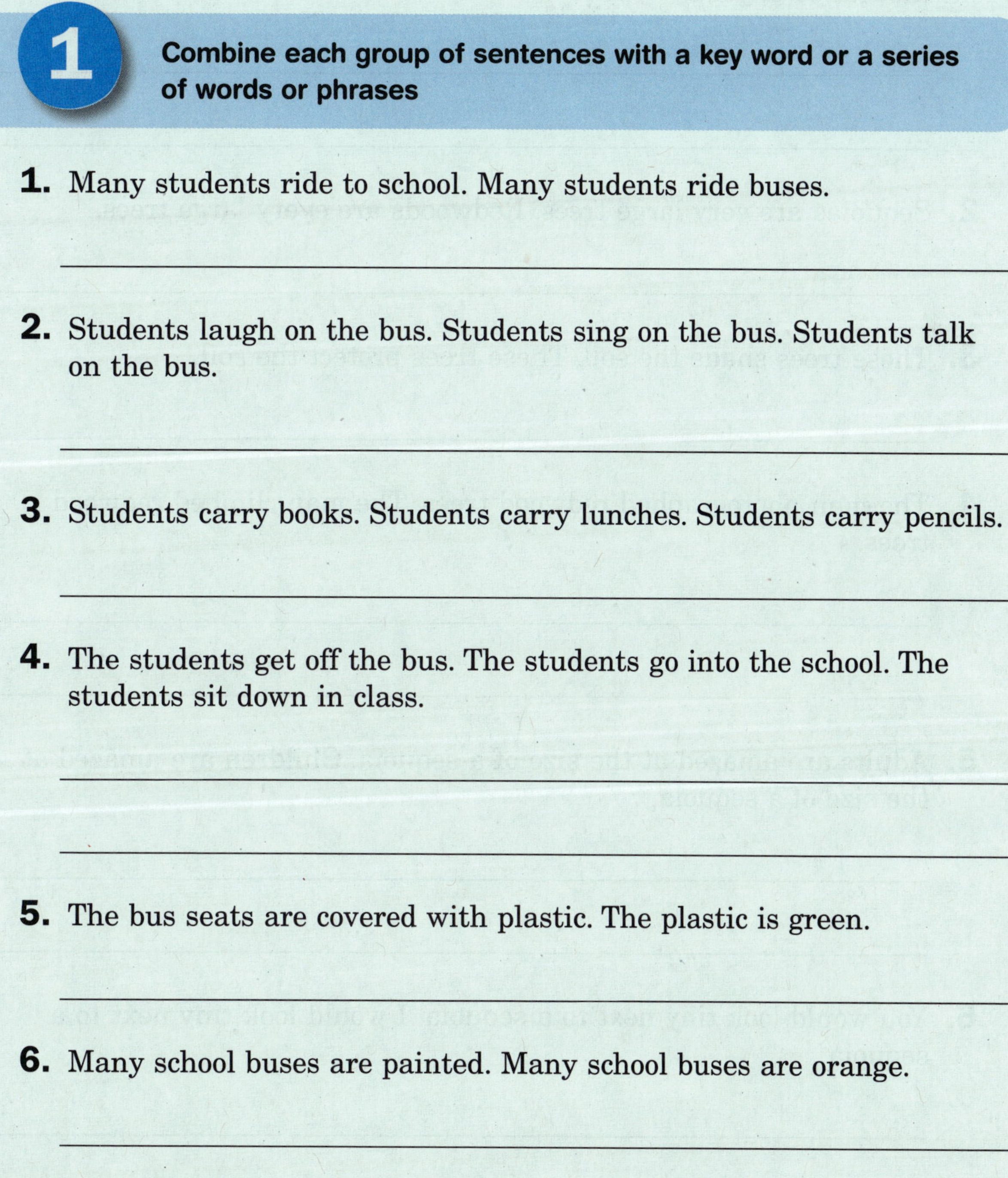

1 Combine each group of sentences with a key word or a series of words or phrases

1. Many students ride to school. Many students ride buses.

____

2. Students laugh on the bus. Students sing on the bus. Students talk on the bus.

____

3. Students carry books. Students carry lunches. Students carry pencils.

____

4. The students get off the bus. The students go into the school. The students sit down in class.

____

____

5. The bus seats are covered with plastic. The plastic is green.

____

6. Many school buses are painted. Many school buses are orange.

____

____

2 **Combine the groups of sentences using compound subjects and verbs.**

1. Some trees live for thousands of years. Some trees grow for thousands of years.

____

____

2. Sequoias are very large trees. Redwoods are every large trees.

____

3. These trees shade the soil. These trees protect the soil.

____

4. The man photographed redwood trees. The man climbed redwood trees.

____

____

5. Adults are amazed at the size of a sequoia. Children are amazed at the size of a sequoia.

____

____

6. You would look tiny next to a sequoia. I would look tiny next to a sequoia.

____

____

Name ______________________________

Sentence Combining Review 2

Write Source Link
408–410

Combine each group of sentences into one longer sentence. You can do this by moving the underlined words into the first sentence. (Sometimes you need to add the word *and*.)

1. You may have noticed that bears have tails. Their tails are short.

____

2. According to legend, bears once had tails that were long. They had tails that were bushy. They had tails that were beautiful.

____

____

3. Then one day a bear saw a fox. The fox was clever.

____

4. The fox was eating crayfish. He was licking his lips.

____

5. The bear asked the fox how to catch crayfish. The bear was hungry.

____

6. The fox told the bear to chop a hole in the ice. He told the bear to put his tail in the hole.

____

____

2

Continue combining the two sentences into one longer sentence. You can do this by moving the underlined words into the first sentence. (Sometimes you need to add the word *and*.)

1. The fox told the bear to sit and wait. He told the bear to wait <u>until a crayfish grabbed his tail</u>.

2. The bear went down to the frozen river. <u>The fox</u> went, too.

3. The bear followed the fox's instructions. The bear was <u>trusting</u>.

4. The ice froze around the bear's tail. It froze <u>quickly</u>.

5. The bear had to leave his tail in the ice. The ice was <u>thick</u>.

6. That is why bears have tails that are short. Their tails are <u>stubby</u>. Their tails are <u>not beautiful</u>.

Next Step **On your own paper, write three short sentences telling what you think of the fox in this story. Then see if you can combine two or more of your sentences to make a longer sentence.**

3 Language Activities

The activities in this section are related to the eight parts of speech. All of the activities have a page link to *Write Source*.

Nouns	117
Pronouns	125
Verbs	133
Adjectives	151
Adverbs	159
Prepositions	163
Conjunctions	165
Transitions	166
Review	167

Name ______________________________

Nouns

A **noun** names a person, a place, a thing, or an idea. The following lists are singular nouns that belong to each of the four groups. A singular noun names just one person, place, thing, or idea.

Person	Place	Thing	Idea
bride	street	bicycle	joy
boy	pool	flowerpot	truth
friend	school	horse	hope
coach	park	whale	sadness

1 **Complete each sentence below by adding nouns from the lists above. (Your sentences can be as silly as you want to make them.) The first one has been done for you.**

1. The ___bride___ hopped over the ___flowerpot___.
2. My ____________ tells the ____________.
3. The ____________ is in the ____________.
4. A ____________ has lots of ____________.
5. The ____________ sang to the ____________.
6. Look at the ____________ riding a ____________.
7. John told his ____________ to go to the ____________.
8. Myra saw a ____________ on the ____________ .
9. The ____________ is full of ____________.

2

Draw a line under the two nouns in each of these sentences. The first sentence has been done for you.

1. The clown sings in the bathtub.
2. The gorilla rides a skateboard.
3. The chef cooked a buzzard.
4. That kid lives in Overshoe.
5. The cowboy roped a skunk.
6. Sarah sang with joy.
7. This path leads to the cave.
8. Mary dreamed of flying cows.
9. The runner has lots of hope.

Next Step **Draw a picture for one of the sentences you worked with in this activity. Talk about your picture with a partner using at least three singular nouns.**

Name ______________________________

Common and Proper Nouns

- A **common noun** names any person, place, thing, or idea.

  man **country** **book**

- A **proper noun** names a specific person, place, thing, or idea.

  Mr. Taylor **Mexico** **Write Source**

1 **Match each group of proper nouns to a common noun. The first one has been done for you.**

	Common Nouns		Proper Nouns
h	**1.** states	**a.**	Canada, Mexico, United States
____	**2.** songs	**b.**	Venus, Mars, Earth
____	**3.** countries	**c.**	Lake Michigan, Great Salt Lake, Lake Okeechobee
____	**4.** mountains	**d.**	Steve, John, Jim
____	**5.** lakes	**e.**	Rocky Mountains, Blue Ridge Mountains, Ozark Mountains
____	**6.** boys	**f.**	"The Star-Spangled Banner," "America the Beautiful," "This Land Is Your Land"
____	**7.** planets	**g.**	Missouri River, Snake River, Yukon River
____	**8.** languages	**h.**	Hawaii, Alaska, California
____	**9.** rivers	**i.**	English, Spanish, Mandarin Chinese
____	**10.** books	**j.**	*Write on Track, Strega Nona, Where the Wild Things Are*

2

After each common noun, write a proper noun that goes with it. Your proper nouns can name real people, places, and things, or they can be made-up names.

Common Nouns	Proper Nouns
1. doctor	______________
2. cat	______________
3. park	______________
4. book	______________
5. store	______________
6. girl	______________
7. team	______________
8. city	______________
9. river	______________
10. movie	______________
11. boy	______________
12. teacher	______________

Next Step **On your own paper, write a paragraph using some of the nouns above. After you finish, label each common noun *C* and each proper noun *P*. Then choose a few more common and proper nouns. Use them to tell a partner a few sentences on a topic of your choice.**

Name ______________________________

Singular and Plural Nouns

- A **singular noun** names one person, place, thing, or idea.

  farmer **park** **car** **freedom**

Write two more singular nouns here.

______________________ ______________________

- A **plural noun** names more than one person, place, thing, or idea.

  farmers **parks** **cars** **freedoms**

Write two more plural nouns here.

______________________ ______________________

Draw one line under each noun in the sentences below. Label each singular noun *S* and each plural noun *P*. The first one has been done for you.

1. My children (P) work in the theater (S).
2. Elizabeth acts in plays.
3. Her brother paints the sets.
4. The theater is on Hill Street.
5. Two new shows just opened.
6. Sean had free tickets.
7. The audience laughed at the jokes.

2 Write five singular nouns in the first column. Then write the plural of each noun in the second column.

	singular	plural
1.	______	______
2.	______	______
3.	______	______
4.	______	______
5.	______	______

Write an interesting sentence using a singular noun from your list. Then tell a partner an interesting sentence using another singular noun from your list.

______

______

Write an interesting sentence using a plural noun from your list. Then tell a partner an interesting sentence using another plural noun from your list.

______

______

Name ______________________________

Possessive Nouns 1

A possessive noun is a noun that shows ownership. To make a singular noun possessive, add an apostrophe and an "s." (Singular means one.)

The tree **frog's** skin is rough and green.

My **teacher's** aquarium holds two frogs.

1 **Circle each possessive noun. Underline what belongs to it. The first one has been done for you.**

1. The frog lives on the pond's shore.
2. Frog eggs float on the water's edge.
3. Tadpoles hatch from a frog's eggs.
4. A tadpole's color changes as it grows.
5. A frog can balance on a tree's leaf.
6. Pet frogs need the owner's care.
7. Mr. Juarez's tank is a mini jungle.

Change the following words into singular possessive nouns.

1. rock a ________________ color
2. mountain that ________________ peak

Name ______________________

Write Source Link
377, 534

Possessive Nouns 2

The plural possessive is used to show ownership. Add an apostrophe after the *s* of most plural nouns to make them possessive.

Chorus frogs' songs sound like a choir.

1 **Circle the correct word in parentheses to finish each sentence below.**

1. You will hear the *(peeper's, peepers')* voices first in the spring.
2. In some places, *(coyote's, coyotes')* howls join in.
3. *(Owl's, Owls')* hoots add to the nightly concerts.
4. Hundreds of *(cricket's, crickets')* songs ring out, too.

2 **Fill in the plural possessive nouns in the chart below.**

	Noun	Singular Possessive Noun	Plural Possessive Noun
1.	boat	boat's	
2.	tree	tree's	
3.	forest	forest's	
4.	lake	lake's	

Name

Personal Pronouns 1

A **pronoun** is a word that takes the place of a noun.

Sam wrote a letter and mailed it.
(The pronoun *it* replaces the noun *letter*.)

Sam opened the mailbox, and he found a letter from Andy.
(The pronoun *he* replaces the noun *Sam*.)

Common Personal Pronouns

Singular Pronouns	Plural Pronouns
I, me, my, mine	we, our, us, ours
you, your, yours	you, your, yours
he, him, his, hers	they, their, them, theirs
she, her, it, its	

In each sentence below, change the crossed-out names to a personal pronoun. The first one has been done for you.

1. Tracy and Gaby started a newspaper, and ~~Tracy and Gaby~~ they write all the stories.

2. Gaby uses ~~Gaby's~~ mom's computer.

3. Tracy and Gaby interviewed the teacher, and ~~the teacher~~ told ~~Tracey and Gaby~~ about her new piano.

4. The teacher told Tracy and Gaby about ~~the teacher's~~ music lessons.

5. The girls like the idea that ~~the girls'~~ teacher is learning new things.

6. Gaby said, "~~Tracy and Gaby~~ like our teacher a lot."

Circle the correct personal pronoun in parentheses for each sentence. The first one has been done for you.

1. Jerome told the girls about *(her, his)* teacher.
2. Jerome said *(his, he)* reading teacher is a soccer coach.
3. The teacher coaches when *(he, him)* is done with school.
4. *(His, ours)* team is happy to have a fair coach.
5. Jerome and Andre learn from *(them, their)* coach.
6. He teaches *(their, them)* to be good sports.

Next Step Write four sentences about a class or a teacher you enjoy. Underline the personal pronouns in your sentences.

Name ______________________

Personal Pronouns 2

A **pronoun** is a word that replaces a noun.

In each of the sentences, write the name of the person that the underlined pronoun stands for. Write Lori or Pam.

One day Lori was playing kickball in the backyard.

1. After a few minutes, she heard Pam calling her.

   ______________ ______________

2. Pam was calling from her yard, but Lori couldn't see her.

   ______________ ______________

3. Lori called, "Do you want to play kickball with me?"

   ______________ ______________

4. "I sure do," answered Pam. And she ran right over.

   ______________ ______________

Fill in personal pronouns for the next part of the story.

Lori and Pam had lots of fun. When ______________ finished playing kickball, the girls went into the house. Lori's mom gave ______________ a treat. Pam said, "Thank ______________. ______________ sure had fun at ______________ house today."

3 **Circle all of the pronouns you find in this paragraph. (There are 19 pronouns all together.)**

Living with a Little Brother

Living with (my) little brother can be hard. First, he tries to copy me. If I have a second glass of milk, he does, too. Second, he always wants to play with my friends. If we play basketball, he wants to join in. But he is too small. Third, he wants to stay up as long as I do. He always says to my mom, "But Tim gets to stay up later." My mom says that he looks up to me, and I should be proud to be his big brother.

Next Step **Write a short paragraph about someone in your family. Circle all of the pronouns you use.**

Name ________________________________

Write Source Link 379

Pronouns: I and Me, They and Them

A **pronoun** is a word that replaces a noun. *I* and *me* are pronouns. *They* and *them* are also pronouns.

I **is used as the subject of a sentence.**

I lost the key.

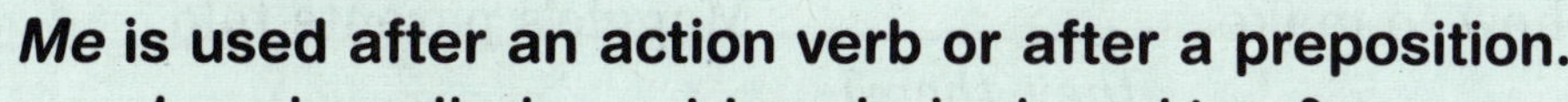

Me **is used after an action verb or after a preposition.**

Angelo called me. Mom baked cookies for me.

They **is used as the subject of a sentence.**

They are friends.

Them **is used after an action verb or after a preposition.**

The lightning scares them. Sophie had a surprise for them.

1

Write the correct word, *I* or *me*, in each blank.

1. ________ need a haircut.
2. Daniel called ________.
3. Janelle asked ________ for a marker.
4. ________ finished my homework.
5. Carla did my chores for ________.

2

Write the correct word, *they* or *them*, in each blank.

1. I invited ________ to my party.
2. ________ like to read stories.
3. I visit ________ every Saturday.
4. We made a present for ________.
5. ________ are my cousins.

3 **Choose the correct word from each pair and write it in the blank.**

_____________ made two bracelets and gave _____________ to
(I, Me) (they, them)

Maggie. _____________ are made from glass beads. My sister showed
(They, Them)

_____________ how to make _____________. Maggie's parents told
(I, me) (they, them)

_____________ the bracelets were very pretty. _____________ said
(I, me) (They, Them)

_____________ should keep making _____________. _____________
(I, me) (they, them) (They, Them)

said _____________ could sell _____________ at the craft show.
(I, me) (they, them)

4 **Write three sentences about a game you play with a friend. Use as many pronouns as you can.**

1. ____

____

2. ____

____

3. ____

____

Name ______________________________

Possessive Pronouns

A **possessive pronoun** shows ownership. It can be used before a noun.

Our street has a new name.

My street is now called King Drive.

1 Choose a word from the list below to complete each sentence. Use each word only once.

my your his her its our their

1. The house at 410 Oak Street is ________________ house.
2. That's ________________ house on the corner.
3. Matt rides ________________ skateboard around the block.
4. Our neighbors painted ________________ house yellow.
5. Mrs. Acker has a gravel driveway at ________________ house.
6. The house is big, and three cars can fit in ________________ garage.
7. What does ________________ house look like?

2 Write about your neighborhood. Use at least three words from the list above in your sentences.

____

3 Finish each sentence with the best choice from the list below.

theirs yours his hers ours mine

1. This journal is ______________.
2. Tom put a picture of a galaxy on ______________ journal's cover.
3. Sherrie has stickers on ______________.
4. Tim and I share this basket of pencils. It is ______________.
5. Another group has a basket of markers. It is ______________.
6. Take this pencil if it is ______________ .

Next Step Write two sentences about items that belong to other people. Use two possessive pronouns from the list above. Then use two different possessive pronouns to tell a partner about items that belong to you or your family.

1. ____

____

2. ____

____

Name ______________________________

Action and Linking Verbs

- An **action verb** tells what the subject does or did.

  Ripe apples drop off trees.

  I ate a piece of apple pie.

- A **linking verb** links the subject to a word in the predicate.

  Apples are fruit.

  That apple pie was delicious!

1 Write an action verb in each sentence.

1. Apple trees ______________________ in late spring.

2. I ______________________ apples in the fall.

3. Once I ______________________ a worm in an apple.

4. My mom ______________________ apple butter.

2 Write a linking verb in each sentence.

1. Applesauce ______________________ soft and delicious.

2. Granny Smith apples ______________________ green.

3. I ______________________ an apple fan!

4. Last year, the orchard ______________________ full of apples.

3

Draw two lines under the verb in each sentence. Write an *A* in the blank if the verb shows action or an *L* if the verb links two words. The first one has been done for you.

A **1.** Johnny Appleseed learned about apples.

_____ **2.** Johnny Appleseed's real name was John Chapman.

_____ **3.** Johnny walked through the Midwest.

_____ **4.** He wore a sack as a shirt.

_____ **5.** He planted many, many apple trees.

_____ **6.** Johnny Appleseed was well-known.

_____ **7.** Many people wrote books about him.

_____ **8.** Some books about Johnny Appleseed are tall tales.

Next Step **Write three sentences about apples. Use at least one of the verbs below in each sentence.**

eat peel chop cut taste is be are was slice

1. ______________________________

____

2. ______________________________

____

3. ______________________________

____

Name ______________________________

Write Source Link

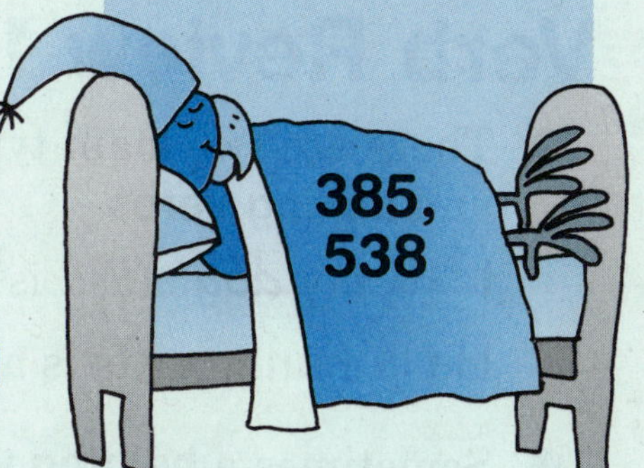

Helping Verbs

A **helping verb** comes before the main verb and helps to state an action or show time.

Helping Verbs: **can, could, did, do, had, has, have, may, should, will, would**

Draw two lines under the helping verb and action verb in each sentence. The first one has been done for you.

1. Parrots can sleep standing up.
2. Humpback whales do make a lot of noise.
3. Australians have named baby kangaroos "joeys."
4. A baby elephant will grow quickly.
5. Swans do eat plants, insects, and small fish.

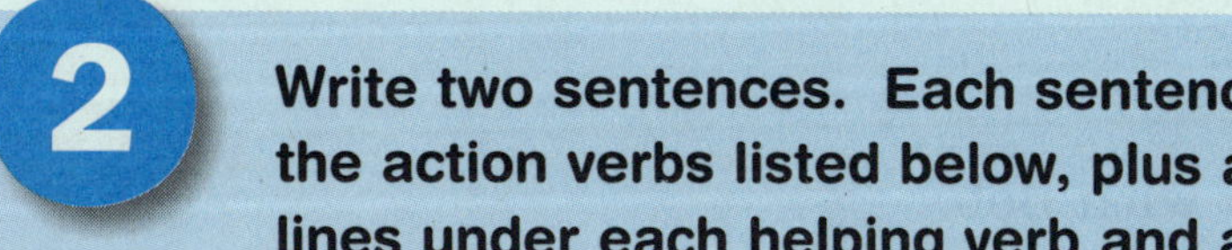

Write two sentences. Each sentence should contain one of the action verbs listed below, plus a helping verb. Draw two lines under each helping verb and action verb.

run **push** **eat** **called**

Example: An elephant can eat a lot.

1. ______________________________

____

2. ______________________________

____

Name ______________________________

Write Source Link
383–385, 538

Verb Review 1

- There are two main types of verbs, **action verbs** and **linking verbs**.
  I fed my dog. (*Fed* is an action verb.)
  He is hungry. (*Is* is a linking verb.)
- Sometimes a **helping verb** is used with an action verb or a linking verb.
  My dog will eat anything.

Draw two lines under the main verb in each sentence. Write an *A* in the blank if the verb shows action or an *L* if the verb links two words. The last two sentences contain helping verbs. For those sentences, underline the helping verbs along with the main verbs.

A 1. My dog runs fast.

_____ 2. My dog acts like a person.

_____ 3. His name is Bob.

_____ 4. We are so happy with Bob.

_____ 5. He plays in the kitchen.

_____ 6. My baby sister Nina loves Bob.

_____ 7. She sits in the kitchen with him.

_____ 8. Once she tasted Bob's dog food.

_____ 9. Nina should eat her own food!

_____ 10. Bob will be our friend forever.

Name

Verb Tenses 1

- A verb in the **present tense** tells you that the action takes place now, or that it happens all the time.

  I hear a cricket singing.

  A cricket hops across the lawn.

- A verb in the **past tense** tells you that the action happened in the past.

  Yesterday a cricket hopped onto my leg.

1 **Carefully read each sentence. Write "present" in the blank if the underlined verb is in the present tense, or "past" if it is in the past tense.**

present 1. Crickets sing by rubbing their wings together.

_______ 2. My grandfather keeps a singing cricket in a cage.

_______ 3. It tells the temperature.

_______ 4. On hot days it chirps fast.

_______ 5. I heard the cricket chirp a few minutes ago.

_______ 6. It chirped 50 times in 15 seconds.

_______ 7. I tried to chirp myself.

_______ 8. I sounded really stupid.

_______ 9. Chirping gives me a sore throat.

2 Each present-tense verb in the following sentences is underlined. On each blank, write the past tense of the verb. Then read the sentence with the new verb in it.

	Present Tense	Past Tense
1.	My friends find crickets in the spring.	found
2.	Sometimes they keep them as pets.	__________
3.	On cold days, the crickets chirp slowly.	__________
4.	My friends and I like bugs.	__________
5.	We see the bug display at the museum.	__________
6.	The largest bug hisses loudly.	__________
7.	It grows to about four inches long.	__________
8.	I enjoy studying insects	__________

Next Step Tell a partner two sentences about insects. Use a present-tense verb in one sentence and a past-tense verb in the other. Then write your sentences on the lines below.

Present tense: ____________________

____

Past tense: ____________________

____

Name ______________________________

Verb Tenses 2

Write Source Link

- Remember that a verb in the **present tense** tells you that the action takes place now, or that it happens all the time.

  It snows.

  I make a snowman.

- A verb in the **future tense** tells you that the action will take place at a later time.

  The sun will come out.

  It will melt the snow.

After each sentence, check whether the underlined verb is in the present tense or in the future tense. The first one has been done for you.

	PRESENT	FUTURE
1. I see snow falling.	✓	
2. Snow falls softly and silently.		
3. It covers roads and roofs.		
4. I hope that it snows all night.		
5. Then they will close the schools.		
6. I will have to shovel snow.		
7. I will clear the walk.		
8. Then I will build a snow fort.		
9. That sounds like fun!		

2

Draw two lines under the verb in each sentence. Write "present" in the blank if the verb is in the present tense, "future" if it is in the future tense.

future **1.** What will melt snow?

_______ **2.** Salt melts snow.

_______ **3.** Dan's experiment will prove it.

_______ **4.** Dan fills two cans with snow or ice.

_______ **5.** He dumps salt on the snow in one can.

_______ **6.** Then he will look at the cans.

Next Step **Change each of the following sentences to the future tense. Write one more sentence about snow. Use the future tense in your new idea. Change the topic to rain and use the future tense as you tell four new sentences to a partner.**

1. Snow falls.

____

2. It clings to branches and twigs.

____

3. Soon the world looks like a giant wedding cake.

____

4. _______________

Name ______________________

Write Source Link

386–387, 540

Verb Tenses 3

The **tense** of a verb tells you if the action happened in the present, past, or future.

Present Tense (happening now):

Peter picks a peck of pickled peppers.

Past Tense (happened before now):

Peter picked a peck of pickled peppers yesterday.

Future Tense (has not happened yet):

Peter will pick a peck of pickled peppers tomorrow.

1 **Draw two lines under the verb in each of the following tongue twisters. Then, in the blank space, write "past," "present," or "future" for the tense of the verb. The first sentence has been done for you.**

past **1.** A big black bug bit a big black bear.

______ **2.** Three gray geese grazed in the green grass.

______ **3.** Teddy took two turtles to Todd's house.

______ **4.** Barbara always burns the brown bread.

______ **5.** A fly flew through the flue.

______ **6.** The dog will choose to chew the shoes.

______ **7.** She will sip a cup of hot cinnamon cider.

______ **8.** I love little lightning bugs.

______ **9.** Carol collects colorful cups.

Present	Past	Future
run	ran	will run
sells	sold	will sell
close	closed	will close
bubbles	bubbled	will bubble
take	took	will take
watch	watched	will watch

2 **Create your own tongue twisters by completing the sentences below. Select verbs from the list above. The first one has been done for you.**

1. The ragged rascal ___ran___ around the rocks.
   (past)

2. She ______________ seashells by the seashore.
   (past)

3. Rosie and Rory ______________ around the roller rink.
   (present)

4. Clyde's Clothes Closet ______________ for cleaning.
   (future)

5. Double bubble gum ______________ double.
   (future)

6. Tim ______________ a turn on Tammy's tandem.
   (past)

7. Wally ______________ the walrus in the water.
   (past)

Next Step **Make up a three tongue twisters to share with a partner. Use a different tense for each one.**

Name ______________________________

Regular Verbs

- Add *-ed* to regular verbs to form the past tense.

  Willy and Milly sailed the boat last summer.

- Also add *-ed* to regular verbs when you use a helping verb such as *has, have,* or *had.*

  Willy had sailed for years.

* * * * * * * * *

- If a regular verb ends in *e*, just add *d* to form the past tense.

  raise ········► raised

- If a one-syllable verb ends in a single consonant, double the consonant and add *-ed.*

  shop ········► shopped

1 Write these regular verbs in the past tense.

1. hop hopped	**9.** push ______
2. hope ______	**10.** save ______
3. name ______	**11.** flip ______
4. tap ______	**12.** splash ______
5. skip ______	**13.** stop ______
6. raise ______	**14.** giggle ______
7. talk ______	**15.** lick ______
8. hum ______	**16.** drip ______

2

In each set of sentences below, study the underlined verb in the first sentence. Then write the *-ed* (past tense) form of the underlined verb to complete the second sentence. The first one has been done for you.

1. They call the boat the *Lilly*.

They ___called___ it the *Lilly* two years ago.

2. Milly and Willy row out to the *Lilly*.

Yesterday, they ________________ out to the *Lilly*.

3. Milly raises the *Lilly's* sail.

Last year, she ________________ it every morning.

4. Milly and Willy love to sail the *Lilly*.

Milly and Willy always have ________________ to sail the *Lilly*.

5. Milly drops the anchor.

Willy gave the signal, and Milly ________________ the anchor.

6. Willy cleans the *Lilly* once a week.

He had ________________ it two days before the storm.

Next Step **Tell a partner sentences using the past tense of *join, close, mail,* and *print*.**

Name ______________________

Singular and Plural Verbs

The subject of a sentence can be singular or plural. Notice how the verb *plays* changes when the subject changes from singular to plural. A single subject must have a single verb. A plural subject must have a plural verb. This is called subject-verb agreement.

Caleb plays basketball at the park. (singular verb)

His friends play with him. (plural verb)

1 Write the correct form of the verb in each sentence.

1. practices practice

Jake, Caleb, and Rhonda ______________ shooting baskets every day.

Sometimes Jake even ______________ at night.

2. dribbles dribble

Caleb ______________ the ball across the court.

Then Jake and Rhonda ______________ it.

3. tosses toss

Rhonda ______________ the ball, and she misses.

Caleb and Jake ______________ and miss.

4. jumps jump

The boys ______________ for the rebound.

Rhonda ______________ , too.

2 Write your own sentences using the singular and plural verbs listed.

1. passes pass

2. scores score

3. cheers cheer

4. joins join

5. chooses choose

Next Step Tell a partner two simple sentences using the singular and plural verbs above. A simple sentence has one complete thought. Make sure that you use correct subject-verb agreement.

Name ______________________________

Irregular Verbs

Study the present and past forms of the irregular verbs in the handbook. As a class, complete the sentences below with the correct forms of the irregular verb.

1. *begin*

present: I ______________ school at 8:30.

past: Last year, school ______________ at 8:00.

past with *had*: When I got there, school had ______________.

2. *am*

present: I ______________ in the third grade.

past: Last year, I ______________ in second grade.

past with *have*: I have ______________ looking forward to third grade.

3. *catch*

present: I ______________ a lot of balls at softball practice.

past: In my last game, I ______________ a fly ball.

past with *had*: I had ______________ two fly balls in other games.

4. *hide*

present: I ______________ from my brother sometimes.

past: Last night, I ______________ in my closet.

past with *have*: I have ______________ there before.

2 Now complete the following sets of sentences on your own. The directions are the same as in part 1.

1. fly

present: I ______________ to Minneapolis every summer.

past: Last year, I ______________ by myself.

past with *have:* I have ______________ for years with my dad.

2. *come*

present: Most days, I ______________ to school with my sister.

past: Yesterday, I ______________ by myself.

past with *have:* I have ______________ by myself two other times.

3. throw

present: I ______________ practice pitches every Friday.

past: Last Friday, I ______________ 30 pitches.

past with *had:* I had ______________ 25 pitches before I hurt my arm.

Next Step **Write two sentences of your own using different forms of the verb *speak*.**

1. ____

____

2. ____

Name ______________________________

Verb Review 2

An **action verb** tells what someone or something does.

Jenny hits lots of home runs.

The wind blows down our fort.

List three action verbs below. Trade papers with a partner. Then write two sentences for each of your partner's action verbs—one singular and one plural.

1. Action verb: ______________________________
Sentence with singular verb:

____

Sentence with plural verb:

____

2. Action verb: ______________________________
Sentence with singular verb:

____

Sentence with plural verb:

____

3. Action verb: ______________________________
Sentence with singular verb:

____

Sentence with plural verb:

____

2 **In the paragraph below, change each underlined verb to past tense. The first one has been done for you.**

rang

Dennis rings the doorbell and then runs away and hides. I see him and tell my mom. She says Dennis does it because he likes me. Maybe she is right. Dennis also rides his bike past our house and brings our newspaper to the door.

Next Step **Write some more sentences about Dennis, using the verbs given. First write a sentence in the present tense. Then write a sentence in the past tense. Then tell a partner two sentences about Dennis using the past and present tenses.**

1. Verb: *write*

Sentence in present tense: ______________________

____

Sentence in past tense: ______________________

____

2. Verb: *go*

Sentence in present tense: ______________________

____

Sentence in past tense: ______________________

____

Name ___________________________

Write Source Link
389, 546

Adjectives 1

- An **adjective** is a part of speech that usually comes before the noun it describes.

  Carrie planted tiny seeds.

  What noun does the adjective *tiny* describe in this sentence? seeds

- Sometimes an **adjective** comes after a linking verb.

  The seeds were tiny.

  What noun does the adjective *tiny* describe in this sentence? seeds

Underline the adjective in each sentence. Then draw an arrow to the noun it describes. (Don't include the words *a, an,* or *the.*) The first one has been done for you.

1. She used a sharp spade to dig.
2. Carrie planted red zinnias.
3. She watered the little seeds.
4. Green leaves soon popped up.
5. Bright sun shone on the plants.
6. Gentle rain watered them.
7. Fat buds formed.
8. Soon Carrie could pick a pretty bouquet of zinnias.

2

Draw a line under each adjective in the following sentences. Then draw an arrow to the noun it describes. All of these adjectives come after a linking verb. The first one has been done for you.

1. Roses are red.
2. Violets are blue.
3. Sugar is sweet.
4. Words are true.
5. Daisies are white.
6. Marigolds are yellow.
7. Honey is sweet.
8. Sarah sure is mellow.

Next Step **Write a sentence for the first three adjective-noun pairs. Then tell a partner a sentence for the fourth pair.**

Adjectives		Nouns
fluffy	→	kitten
tough	→	guy
beautiful	→	song
silver	→	earrings

1. ______________________________

____

2. ______________________________

____

3. ______________________________

____

Name ______________________

Write Source Link
384, 389

Adjectives 2

An **adjective** is a part of speech that describes a noun or a pronoun.

A **descriptive** adjective describes something.

Texas has many beautiful sites.

(*Beautiful* is a descriptive adjective that describes Texas.)

An **limiting** adjective tells *which one, how many,* or *whose.*

This state has many beautiful sights.

(*This* is a limiting adjective that tells which one.

Circle the limiting adjectives in the sentences below.

1. This is my favorite time of year.
2. Our Texas weather is cool and sunny in the fall.
3. The perfect weather lasts for about three months.
4. The trees begin to lose their green color.
5. We really enjoy that hayride every October.
6. I'm sorry that your weather is already cold by now.

Next Step **Think of your favorite time of year. Use a limiting adjective in a sentence describing that season.**

____

____

Adjectives 3

Write Source Link
389

The **articles** *a, an,* and *the* are **adjectives.**

A full moon is an amazing sight at the seashore.
(*A, an,* and *the* are all articles.)

Underline each article in the sentences below. The sentences may have one or two articles.

1. Every animal has a pulse rate.
2. It is measured by the number of heartbeats in a minute.
3. A big animal's pulse rate is slower than a small animal's.
4. An average person's heart beats 72 times per minute.
5. A mouse can have a pulse rate of over 500 beats per minute.
6. A runner's pulse rate may be only 35 beats per minute.

Next Step **Write one sentence that includes two articles. Then tell a partner a sentence that uses a different article.**

Name ________________________________

Proper Adjectives

An adjective formed from a proper noun is called a **proper adjective**.

America has a flag.
(*America* is a proper noun.)

The American flag is red, white, and blue.
(*American* is an adjective that describes the flag.)

Circle the proper adjectives in the sentences below.

1. The English language contains words from many places.
2. *Medicine* is a French word.
3. A German teacher created the word *kindergarten*.
4. The word *pretzel* comes from the German language.
5. *Moose, chipmunk,* and *opossum* are Native American words.
6. The Scandinavian people first used the word *egg*.
7. *Chimpanzee* and *banana* are words from African countries.

Next Step **Think of a food that comes from another country. Use a proper adjective in a sentence describing that food.**

____

____

Name ______________________

Write Source Link
546

Compound Adjectives

A **compound adjective** is made up of more than one word. Some compound adjectives are spelled as one word. Some words are spelled with a hyphen.

We got drinks at the **drive-up** window.

1

Match the following words to create compound adjectives. Write them on the lines.

______________	**1.** house	color
______________	**2.** old	fashioned
______________	**3.** hard	mother's
______________	**4.** grand	ware
______________	**5.** water	hold

2

Fill in each blank with the best choice from the words you created above.

1. Roseanna visits her ______________ house in summer.

2. Grandma Maria lives next to the ______________ store.

3. Roseanna helps Grandma with ______________ chores.

4. Roseanna loves Grandma's big, ______________ couch.

5. Over the couch is a giant ______________ painting of a forest.

Name ________________________________

Forms of Adjectives

Adjectives have three different forms.

Positive: This pebble is small.

Comparative: This pebble is smaller than that rock.

Superlative: This pebble is the smallest stone in my collection.

Write sentences for the forms of the adjectives listed below.

loud, louder, loudest

1. ______________________________

2. ______________________________

____

3. ______________________________

____

happy, happier, happiest

1. ______________________________

2. ______________________________

____

3. ______________________________

____

2 **Write a paragraph about a beautiful or interesting place you have visited. Use plenty of adjectives in your writing.**

Next Step **Circle the adjectives in your paragraph. Did you write any adjectives in the comparative (ending in *-er*) or the superlative form (ending in *-est*)?**

Name ______________________

Adverbs 1

An **adverb** is a word that describes a verb in time, in place, or in manner. Adverbs usually tell *when, where,* or *how.*

- Some adverbs that tell *when:*

  always never soon weekly

- Some adverbs that tell *where:*

  outside there up

- Some adverbs that tell *how:*

  slowly loudly jokingly

1 **Circle the adverb in each sentence. Then write whether it tells *when, where, or how.* The first one has been done for you.**

1. Jeremy (always) eats his cabbage. when
2. Karen goes to bed early. ______________
3. Rags comes quickly when he is called. ______________
4. Shari never teases her little brother. ______________
5. Todd goes to the dentist cheerfully. ______________
6. Michelle cleans her room daily. ______________
7. I took the trash outside. ______________
8. Sean makes his bed carefully. ______________
9. Emily comes here for lunch. ______________

2 **Cross out the adverb in each sentence. Replace it with a different adverb that changes the meaning of the sentence. The first one has been done for you.**

1. "I'll ride a bike," Mom said ~~seriously.~~ jokingly
2. Sparky snores softly.
3. Cal seldom sees his cousins.
4. Tamika did her chores happily.
5. Maria is never late for school.
6. "Those boys are playing so quietly," said Granddad.
7. Fuzzy stays nearby when he knows it's bath time.

Next Step **Write three sentences about yourself. Then tell a partner three different sentences about yourself using different adverbs.**

1. Use the adverb *someday* (when).

____

2. Use the adverb *outside* (where).

____

3. Use the adverb *slowly* (how).

____

Name ______________________________

Adverbs 2

An **adverb** is a word that describes a verb in time, in place, or in manner. Adverbs usually answer *when* (adverb of time), *where* (adverb of place), or *how* (adverb of manner).

1

Adverbs of time tell *when* or *how often* an action is done. Fill in the blank in each sentence with one adverb from the list below.

yesterday	soon	now	first
tomorrow	later	weekly	last

1. Our class went to the toy museum ______________________.
2. I hope we can go back again ______________________.
3. In fact, I wish we could go ______________________.

2

Adverbs of place tell *where* something happens. Fill in the blank in each sentence with one adverb from the list below.

inside	here	up
outside	there	down

1. I told my mom I wanted to go ______________________ to play.
2. She looked ______________________ at me.
3. "Why don't you just play ______________________?" she asked.

3 **Adverbs of manner tell *how* something is done. Fill in the blank in each sentence with one adverb from the list below.**

quietly	carefully	slowly	happily
loudly	carelessly	quickly	sadly

1. I like to play my cassette player ______________.
2. When I clean up my room, I do it very ______________.
3. When it's time to eat, my cat comes running ______________.

Next Step **Write four adverbs. Then write a paragraph that has all four adverbs in it. Choose four new adverbs. Use these adverbs to tell a partner about something you like to do.**

1. ______________ 3. ______________

2. ______________ 4. ______________

____

____

____

____

____

____

____

Name

Prepositions and Prepositional Phrases

A **preposition** is a word that can show direction or position. A phrase that begins with a preposition and ends with a noun is called a **prepositional phrase.**

prepositions: *to, with*
prepositional phrases:
to the lighthouse, under the bridge

Draw a line under the prepositional phrase in each sentence below. Then circle each preposition. The first one has been done for you.

1. Ray was in deep water.
2. Ray was swimming against the tide.
3. He went backward with every stroke.
4. Waves washed over his head.
5. He was not near the beach.
6. Just then, he felt the nudge of a boat.
7. A lifeguard threw him a life preserver on a rope.
8. Ray reached for the rope.
9. The lifeguard rowed Ray toward the beach.
10. Ray said, "Thank you. I was really in danger."

2

Draw a line under the prepositional phrases in the sentences below. Then circle each preposition. (Some of these sentences have more than one prepositional phrase. In this case, notice that each prepositional phrase ends with the noun the preposition refers to.) The first one has been done for you.

1. Pay attention to these rules about water safety.
2. Swim at beaches protected by lifeguards.
3. Never jump into strange waters.
4. Always look for underwater obstacles.
5. Do not swim in unmarked areas or in bad weather.
6. Always swim close to the shore and with a friend.
7. Go slowly into cold water.
8. Swim with other people.
9. Stay inside the buoys.

Next Step **Create a sign for one of the safety rules above. Describe your picture to partner using prepositions and prepositional phrases.**

Name ___________________

Conjunctions

A **conjunction** connects words or groups of words. The most common conjunctions are *and, but,* and *or.* There are three conjunctions in the following sentence:

Charley and Barbara wore their coats and hats, but they forgot their boots.

1

Draw a circle around the 10 conjunctions in this story.

The Sun and the Wind

Who is stronger, the sun or the wind? Well, once upon a time, each one thought it was stronger, so they had a contest.

"I am strong enough to make that man take off his hat, his scarf, and his coat," bragged the wind. The sun said nothing. It just hid behind a cloud.

The wind blew and blew, but the man did not take off his hat, his scarf, or his coat. Instead, he pulled them tighter and tighter to his body.

Then the sun came out brightly but quietly. Soon the man grew warm. He took off his hat, and he took off his scarf. Then he removed his coat.

Now do you know who is stronger? Is it the sun or the wind?

Next Step **Write a sentence that answers the last two questions in the story. Then use coordinating conjunctions to tell a partner what you thought of the story.**

Name ______________________________

Write Source Link
458

Transitions

Transitions are words that signal a new, important idea is coming. Transitions help show *time, location,* or *additional information.*

Some transitions show *time:*

first next finally

Some transitions show *location:*

above beside near

Some transitions show *more information:*

again also another

1 **Write the correct transition in each blank.**

behind then nearby first also after

1. The ____________ thing we had to do was decide which kind of pet we wanted.
2. ____________ we decided that a dog would be best for our family.
3. We ____________decided we wanted a rescue dog.
4. We went to the ____________ pet store that has rescue dogs every Saturday.
5. Standing ____________ all these big dogs was a little pup looking right at me.
6. ____________ one look, I knew he was the dog for me.

Next Step **Use transitions to tell a story about something special you have done with your family.**

Name ______________________

Write Source Link
374–395,
532–554

Parts of Speech Review 1

This activity is a review of the parts of speech.

Write three examples of each part of speech. Do as many as you can on your own. Then ask a classmate for help or check *Write Source.*

Nouns
(Name a person, a place, a thing, or an idea)

____
____
____

Possessive Pronouns
(Used before a noun to show ownership)

____
____
____

Verbs
(Show action or link ideas)

____
____
____

Adjectives
(Describe a noun or pronoun)

____
____
____

Adverbs
(Describe a verb; tell how an action is done)

____
____
____

Coordinating Conjunctions
(Connect words or groups of words)

____
____
____

Prepositions
(Introduce a prepositional phrase)

____
____
____

Transitions
(Signal when ideas change)

____
____
____

Next Step In the space below, draw a picture that shows this sentence:

The shiny red spaceship rocketed to the stars!

Copy the sentence under your drawing. Then label each word to show what part of speech it is.

Name ______________________________

Parts of Speech Review 2

Write Source Link
374–395,
532–554

Fill in each blank below with a word that is the correct part of speech. Use each word only once.

in	silently	their	birds	quickly
pointed	they	worms	sharp	and
but	soars	floats	around	finally

1. **Nouns:** Robins are ____________ that fly and eat ____________ .

2. **Pronouns:** Finches eat ____________ seeds until ____________ spot a cat.

3. **Verbs:** A hawk ____________ above, and a duck ____________ in the bay.

4. **Adjectives:** Falcons have ____________ claws and ____________ beaks.

5. **Adverbs:** Owls hunt ____________ and ____________ to catch prey.

6. **Conjunctions:** Barn owls ____________ screech owls sleep all day, ____________ they hunt at night.

7. **Prepositions:** Chickadees live ____________ the northern United States, and they often flock ____________ seed feeders.

8. **Transition:** We____________ reached the beach after a long drive.

2 **Read the following paragraph and follow the directions below.**

My grandmother is a bird-watcher. Grandma Fran and I spend time quietly watching and feeding many birds. First, Grandma always looks at her bird book. Then, she marks what kinds of birds she sees in a notebook. I read her long list and carefully count the different kinds. Dozens of birds eat around Grandma's backyard. Grandpa says Grandma has seen every bird in our state, but I know Grandma can find more. Look! Is that a blue jay or a bluebird? I bet Grandma knows.

Write the underlined words in the correct spaces. Find two examples for each part of speech.

Part of Speech	1	2
noun		
pronoun		
verb		
adjective		
adverb		
conjunction		
preposition		
transition		